CLASSIC PLAYGROUND GAMES

from

Hopscotch *to* Simon Says

by Susan Brewer

REMEMBER WHEN

First published in Great Britain in 2008 by
REMEMBER WHEN
An imprint of
Pen & Sword Books Ltd
47 Church Street
Barnsley
South Yorkshire
S70 2AS

ISBN 978 1 84468 025 2

A CIP catalogue record for this book is
available from the British Library.

Printed and bound in Malta
by Progress Press Co. Ltd.

Pen & Sword Books Ltd incorporates the imprints of Pen & Sword Aviation,
Pen & Sword Maritime, Pen & Sword Military, Wharncliffe Local History,
Pen & Sword Select, Pen & Sword Military Classics, Leo Cooper, Remember When,
Seaforth Publishing and Frontline Publishing

For a complete list of Pen & Sword titles please contact
PEN & SWORD BOOKS LIMITED
47 Church Street, Barnsley, South Yorkshire, S70 2AS, England
E-mail: enquiries@pen-and-sword.co.uk
Website: www.pen-and-sword.co.uk

Contents

Introduction   6

1   School Days – *Playtime Pleasures and Lost Games*   7

2   Favourite Playground Songs – *Oranges and Lemons*   21

3   Sing Song Chants – *With a Knick-knack Paddywhack*   43

4   Rhymes and Puns – *One Potato, Two Potato*   51

5   Games without Props – *Simon Says, "Who Needs a Playstation?"*   63

6   It or He – *You Can't Catch Me!*   81

7   Childhood Nonsense – *I Beg Your Pardon*   85

8   Ball Games – *It's My Ball and I'm Going Home*   91

9   Clapping Games – *Pat-a-cake*   105

10 Skipping and Chants – *Bumps and Grinds*   111

11 Flower Games – *Daisy Chains*   135

12 Playing with Things – *Don't Lose Your Marbles*   137

13 Indoor play – *The Sun Has Got His Mac on*   159

Acknowledgements   187

Photo credits and further reading   188

Index   189

Introduction

I HOPE that this will be a nostalgic wallow for those of us whose school days are many years past, and an inspiration for parents, teachers, child-minders and children seeking different games to play. I also aim to preserve some of the rhymes and games which are becoming lost as children turn to other pursuits. Since I began the research, I have spoken to dozens of children and adults, aged from five to eighty-five, and contacted many libraries, local history societies and newspapers. Additionally, I have received letters, e-mails and phone calls from around Britain from people eager to share their childhood memories. Over and again I hear the same comment, 'Since I started to recall the games I played, I find the chants popping into my head at odd moments'. One lady was stirring the custard when a rhyme suddenly clamoured for attention – she had to grab a pencil and paper and write, while, no doubt, the custard burnt! So, be warned – by the time you have finished reading this book you too will have a head filled with long-forgotten rhymes, but, hopefully, a warm glow in your heart. (And, possibly, a burnt saucepan!).

This isn't intended to be a scholarly slice of research. My book is more of a joyful 'memory-jogger', one to reawaken thoughts of carefree days spent skipping, running and chanting in a school playground; a time when we not only absorbed traditional rhymes and games, but a time, too, when we adapted and altered them to make them fit in with our world. Today, I'm pleased to say, in spite of all the adverse reports, the majority of youngsters still play group games, and still improvise, adapt and ad-lib to bring them up to date.

I have been amazed by the number of 'forbidden' school games, which seem to grow longer every day – many of the pastimes enjoyed by generations of children are in danger of being forgotten, as the 'nanny state' engulfs us all in cotton wool. Amongst the games which have been banned in various British schools over the last few years are: yo-yos, marbles, 'He', French skipping, British Bulldog, handstands, conkers, climbing frames, ball games, hide and seek, marbles – and even daisy chains! However, refreshingly, now some schools are rediscovering the traditional games, teaching children skipping rhymes and chants, showing them how to play bat and ball, marbles and other games which, to children of a previous generation, would have been as natural as breathing. Long may it continue.

The one thing which has really struck me while writing this book is how imaginative children are – new games are still invented, silly rhymes still trip off the tongue. We should feel very proud. For, once, we were children, too.

Susan Brewer

1. School Days

PLAYTIME PLEASURES AND LOST GAMES

FOR MANY children, that first day at school can be traumatic, even though the advent of playschools means that today's youngsters have often already experienced the joys of mixing with other children. Many children now start school part-time at the age of four. Today's children have also become used to being away from their mothers for a few hours as more women are working. Yet the first day in 'big' school is a milestone, one which has entailed days, if not weeks, of preparation. There may have been a school uniform to be bought, and even if not, there will probably be new 'school clothes', gym kit, lunch box and sports shoes needed. The child feels excited, nervous and important in turn, not quite knowing what to expect. Most of us have clear memories of that first day; the very fact that we remember it so well demonstrates the impact it must make at such an early age.

Children coming home from School.

20371

FREEDOM! Late Nineteenth Century school children.

7

Milk time

When I was at school, milk time was a highlight, because it was the prelude to playtime. The quicker we drank our milk, the quicker we could go out to play. We were all given a piece of cardboard with lines of wool attached, and shown how to weave. This was important, because we were making a milk mat, so that we didn't put wet milk bottles on our desks. Of course, we all pulled the wool too tight so our mats had waists, but they were brightly coloured and made our desks look jolly. The milk came in small glass bottles and the caretaker had made a hole in each foil lid to push the paper straw through.

Remember those little glass bottles? They held a third of a pint (200ml) of creamy milk and, for many children, it was the only milk they would get to drink. It was invaluable for their health. At first, the tops were made from cardboard, but later were replaced by foil. Sometimes in summer, the milk was left standing in the sun and became warm and curdled, but we still drank it. In the winter, the caretaker would put the crate by the radiator to warm it up a bit – it never went properly warm, just a bit tepid and tasted horrible. In 1971, a certain Education Secretary decided free milk in all schools was no longer a priority, especially for older children, and so she became known as 'Mrs Thatcher, Milk Snatcher'. Nowadays, less than twenty-five per cent of school children have milk at school.

Playtime

After milk time came playtime. Playtime in the 1950s was quite gentle; sometimes girls would bring in their dolls' prams and push them sedately around the playground. A small group of us were fascinated by a wall in the playground made from soft yellow brick, and were convinced fairies lived in the little holes in the bricks. Bizarrely, we would solemnly scrape up the lumps of chewing gum which dotted the playground and push it into the holes for the fairies. Whether we were feeding them or blocking their escape route, I can't remember!

CARING FOR BABY – Girls with dolls.

The reason there was so much chewing gum around was probably because many shops had a chewing gum machine outside. You put in a penny and turned a knob, and a piece of gum came out. However, every fourth turn produced two pieces of gum – presumably as a way of enticing people to buy more than one piece – and an arrow was helpfully marked on the knob. When the arrow was in a certain place you knew you would get two pieces, a bargain. Many children would chew gum, then spit it out. My friends and I thought that was not only 'rude', it was wasteful, so we swallowed it. So far, I am pleased to report, I have experienced no harmful effects!

Many of us liked to spend time holding onto the 'playground lady' (the lady who kept an eye on the playing children). Sometimes, she might have a dozen little girls attached to her hand, arm or coat. Every so often, we would all halt as a desperate child ran up to plead for a sheet of toilet paper. The toilets were in the playground, and the dinner lady carried a pack of paper around with her. She would carefully peel off a sheet for the needy child – sometimes two, if she felt generous – and then we would proceed with our circuit of the playground. The playground lady was the recipient of all our secrets, and must have had a wonderful time regaling her colleagues later.

A village school in the Nineteenth Century.

Playtime fun
Whilst still in my infant school, I was either playing Cowboys with a lovely little boy called Karl, Mummies and Babies with other dolly-minded girls or, for a while, Mermaids, when we'd pretend that we lived in jewel-encrusted caves under the sea and we'd go 'swimming' around the school playground.

Karen Conn,
devoted Mum from Worcestershire

Playground games

Hopscotch, skipping, marbles, five-stones and He (or tag) were the popular 1950s playground games, as well as chanting games such as Oranges and Lemons or Farmer's in the Dell (see p22). These games would have been known to our parents, grandparents and great-grandparents, who played similar games when they were at school. Some of their pastimes, though, would have been unfamiliar to us. We probably wouldn't have chased after a metal hoop, coaxing it along with a stick. Most of us didn't play with wooden spinning tops which hummed when you whipped them with string tied to a stick, and we didn't all play Squeak Piggy Squeak or act out charades.

TAKING AIM – Marbles.

Imagination was the vital ingredient – we would act out situations. A particular favourite was Mothers and Fathers, which could be played by quite a large group who would take the parts of different adults, children, pets and neighbours. We had a school field at our primary school in Welwyn Garden City, Hertfordshire, and the hedges and low-growing hawthorn trees formed excellent 'houses'. Various chasing games were also played and, if we were really lucky, two of the boys would pick a fight and a glorious scramble would break out as more and more boys joined in, the girls cheering them on. Eventually, of course, a harassed teacher would break up the fight; these fights were never vicious, just outbreaks of high spirits.

Nonsense songs and rhymes were definitely 'in' when we were young; parodies of popular songs, made-up limericks, doggerel verse – they all echoed around the playground, recounted, polished and refined as they were passed from child to child. Unlike today's school playground rhymes, the ones we learnt weren't really rude – also, unlike today, they didn't contain swear words, and certainly four-letter words never cropped up. I can remember a child using the word 'bum' in class and shocking everyone!

Where has childhood gone?
Over the last few years, there have been various surveys and reports regarding the decrease in children's outdoor play. In this modern world of computers, hand-held game consoles, i-pods, DVD players and easily affordable television sets, children often prefer to spend their leisure time watching or playing with an electronic device, rather than following traditional or outdoor pursuits. Games which have been handed down from generation to generation and rhymes which have passed from child to child, are in danger of being lost and forgotten. Whereas a child of a previous generation would enjoy tree climbing, making a camp, digging in a sandpit or sailing a boat on a pond, to the modern child, these attractions are often unknown or impractical. We are all aware of the loss of freedom to today's children when compared to our own childhood. Years ago, children were free to wander, even in fields and woods, on their own or in groups, or could play in the streets in safety. Nowadays, worried parents keep a much tighter rein over their

PLAYTIME.

VICTORIAN PLAYTIME.

children's activities, but, as consolation, shower them with electrical goods and expensive toys to entertain them and, in some cases, to ease the busy parents' conscience.

Forgetting past pleasures

A primary school head in North Wales said that it was necessary to teach some of her new pupils to walk on bumpy grass, as they had never done such a thing before. Their parents had exercised strict control by making them keep to the pavements – imagine children who have never known the sheer joy of running barefoot through dewy grass, or have never strode through a grassy meadow, feeling the tractor ruts, rabbit runs and tangled sedges beneath their feet, or the long feathery grasses tickling their knees as they race through it.

Problems of a different kind are also encountered in the school playground – pupils bring electronic hand-held games to school, or they listen to their i-pods, scorning skipping, chasing and other traditional games. Apart from football, which is still very popular, ball games are less often played, while games involving singing or chanting in a circle are rare, because, as one youngster said, "The big children make fun if we sing those kinds of things". Schools themselves must take some responsibility as many have placed bans on playground games, fearing they might be sued if a child is injured.

Consequently, a recent survey found that traditional school playtime games, such as skipping, conkers, hopscotch, marbles and He are fast disappearing. Instead, children prefer to spend their break times playing with electronic games, chatting or acting out scenes from cartoons and, worryingly, soap operas. It's cool just to hang out and discuss the new fashions, pop groups, TV shows, 'celebs' and the latest trends. Children are no longer working off surplus energy and getting a beneficial amount of exercise; now, they are much more sedentary which, in turn, is leading to problems with obesity.

Less active

Activities which parents remember from their own childhood, such as seaside day trips, harvest festivals, nativity plays, museum visits, school milk breaks, school fêtes – and, of course, traditional playground games – are rapidly becoming a thing of the past. Out of school activities too, such as tree-climbing, building dens, going for walks, cycling and street games, are often not possible for today's children. Most parents won't let their youngsters out of their sight, apart from when they are safe in school; the freedom which previous generations took for granted is, sadly, no longer possible. Society has changed; today's children no longer trust a friendly stranger – not even the local policeman. Adventures undertaken by children such as Enid Blyton's Famous Five are alien to today's generation; most children can't go off for even a few hours on their own, armed just with a jam sandwich and a bottle of pop – or today's equivalent of a tin of cola – let alone spend a few nights in a tent in the middle of a wood!

Tragedy strikes Giant Stride

Fernhurst School, Sussex, circa 1900.

However, school could be a dangerous place – even today, accidents happen; a child can fall from a bench, slip on the playground or skid on a discarded apple core. Nowadays, in this age of compensation awareness, schools are so terrified of being sued that often it seems children are wrapped in cotton wool, with many traditional games now banned. Just over a hundred years ago, in Fernhurst School, Sussex, a particularly tragic accident occurred. According to the Fernhurst School Log Books, 1895-1921, 'On 10 May, 1901, the whole village was shocked by a fatal accident at the school. During playtime that morning, while several children were swinging round the Giant Stride, the pole broke off suddenly and fell upon

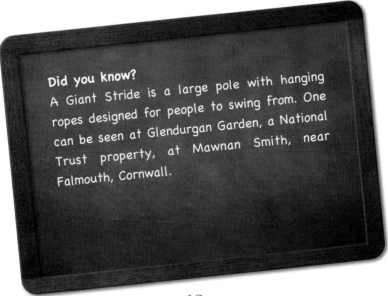

Did you know?
A Giant Stride is a large pole with hanging ropes designed for people to swing from. One can be seen at Glendurgan Garden, a National Trust property, at Mawnan Smith, near Falmouth, Cornwall.

13

one of the children, Ada Rozier (13 years of age) and killed her. One other child, Bessie Ralph, had her arm broken. School was promptly closed for the afternoon, and three days later school was closed during the afternoon so that the children might attend the funeral.'

Giant Stride, formerly at Wicksteed Park, Northamptonshire.

Did you know?

Recently, a British school announced that they were banning 'contact' games from their playground, including He and Kiss Chase. They were also stopping girls from walking around arm in arm (they didn't mention the boys!). The school authorities believed that, by taking this course, they would stop unruly behaviour – but it seems they would also be stopping many traditional games. Other schools have already banned conkers for safety reasons, while marbles have also been outlawed by some schools. How long before they ban skipping ropes (someone might get strangled), chasing games (someone might fall) or hopscotch (dangerous, jumping on one leg. Or someone might eat the chalk...)? Well, actually, all those games have been recently banned too, for one reason or another. It all boils down though to the same thing – the school might be sued if a child is hurt.

PLAYING HOPSCOTCH – mustn't land on the lines!

Regaining traditions

Even so, there is hope – some schools are actively encouraging traditional games to be played at break times, and teaching the children skipping chants and old rhymes. They provide skipping ropes, balls and hoops, and draw out hopscotch grids on the playground. Not only are the children playing together in harmony and learning the meaning of teamwork, they will be remembering all these activities to pass on to the next generation.

SWING YOUR PARTNER.

Why is playtime so important?

Children need to play – play stimulates the senses, which is why wise mothers provide visual, colourful toys right from birth. By the time a child is ready for school, hopefully they will have learnt from their siblings, the children they meet at playschool and through their environment, how to play. Play is so much more than kicking a ball around; it's learning how to share and interact with other children, to co-operate and to care for them. Of course, games such as He, hide and seek, skipping, hopscotch and others also provide physical exercise, which is often lacking today as the majority of children are ferried to school by car or the school bus. Even twenty years ago, most children walked to school but, as roads become busier and stories of child abduction, murder and abuse are reported in the press, parents are reluctant to take risks. In 2007, it was announced that fewer than 10 per cent of primary school children walk to school, as opposed to 80 per cent 35 years ago.

Though games like football provide all-important teamwork, they are not the first choice of every child. It can be seen that, when playing traditional games, children learn to co-operate in a more sociable atmosphere without the aggressive, 'win at all costs' attitude. Games such as hopscotch, hide and seek, skipping, chanting games, marbles and tag encourage co-operation and support but not in a competitive manner. The players need the help of others – skipping, for

> **Yesterday's games**
> Once you moved up to Juniors you had a different playground where we would play games like Kiss Catch, Tig, British Bulldogs, Skipping and, later, Elastics.
>
> Shelley Cuff,
> born 1960, Chorley, Toy Collector

16

example, requires people to turn the rope. Communal games help children not only to play together, but to communicate more during play and, in turn, this has been seen to make bullying less likely. A primary school head teacher said that, since the traditional games were reintroduced into his school, behaviour amongst the pupils had improved, while, as the games required hopping, skipping, jumping and running, the pupils' health also benefited.

Why do schools have playtime?

Playtime for children was instituted because doctors and other specialists decreed that children needed fresh air and exercise. Although children's games have varied and been updated and improvised over the decades, in many ways, they still resemble the games played over a century ago when Victorian schools had 'recreation' periods of about quarter of an hour. Children were allowed into the playground to run, play and work off their energy – they would probably have been confined behind a desk since school began, and fidgeting would not have been condoned. At lunchtime, most children would go home but those who lived too far to walk there and back in the allotted time, usually an hour and a half or even two hours, brought their 'dinner' to school – often a hunk of bread, sometimes with jam or dripping. Then they could play in the playground until afternoon school began.

Past playtimes

My father was Headmaster of the Infants and Junior Schools in Castleford, Yorks. The boys and the girls both had hard playgrounds separated by a wall. Each playground also had a large three-sided, barn-like enclosure in the corner so that we could play undercover when it was wet. It also provided walls for the ball games. The area was very poor – families lived in back-to-back houses with no gardens and the children often came to school with their toes hanging out of their shoes.

Jane High, age 79
'A Yorkshire Lass'

Terror of the Playground

'Neither managers nor teachers like the trouble of exercising supervision over the pupils during the hours of play . . . the consequence is that a spirit of lawlessness often reigns supreme in the playground . . . and the more timid children are kept in a state of terror.'

E.R. Robson, first architect of the London School Board, School Architecture, 1874

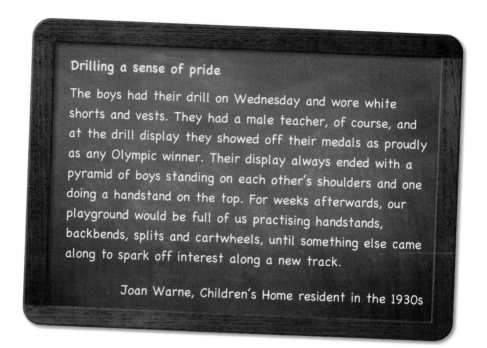

Drilling a sense of pride

The boys had their drill on Wednesday and wore white shorts and vests. They had a male teacher, of course, and at the drill display they showed off their medals as proudly as any Olympic winner. Their display always ended with a pyramid of boys standing on each other's shoulders and one doing a handstand on the top. For weeks afterwards, our playground would be full of us practising handstands, backbends, splits and cartwheels, until something else came along to spark off interest along a new track.

Joan Warne, Children's Home resident in the 1930s

Drill

Sometimes, playtimes became regimented, especially in the early part of the Twentieth Century when the fashion for 'drill' came in. Drill was a form of exercise or 'physical jerks', carried out with the children in regimented rows. On command, they would bend, stretch or windmill their arms. It was a well-intended

Practising drill.

Gymnastics was as easy as standing on your head.

idea as the children were getting exercise. However, occasionally it was substituted for playtime, which in effect meant that children were getting no free time to themselves. Usually, though, drill was a separate item on the school agenda, performed in the school hall or playground, with the children wearing special drill uniforms. Of course, the drill-mania spilled over into playtimes, with children practising exercises, and, especially, climbing on each other to make pyramids or 'boy-heaps' (see p2).

Homemade toys
Unlike today, in our grandparents' era and before, children didn't have more toys than they knew what to do with – if children had toys at all, they would probably have been quite simple playthings. They would also have been treasured, so it was unlikely they would have been taken to school, apart from recreational toys such as hoops and tops.

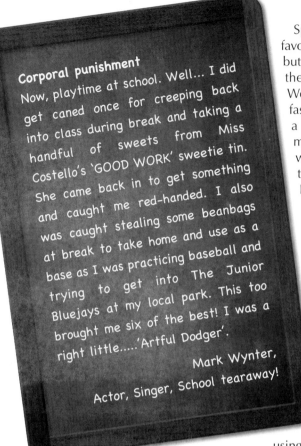

Spinning tops and whips were favourite toys right up until the 1930s, but hoops and sticks lost much of their popularity before the First World War. Makeshift tops could be fashioned by hammering a nail into a cotton reel or similar spool, and metal wheel rims or barrel hoops were perfect for racing, rolling them along with the aid of a stick. Balls were always popular and, in Victorian times, boys would often make do with a pig's bladder, which they would beg from the butcher's shop. They would inflate the bladder, and it made a serviceable football. Footballs could also be made from bundles of old rags, tightly bound with string. Pieces of wood made bats, sometimes the wood was roughly shaped to form a cricket bat with a handle. Skittles were a favourite, and a makeshift game could easily be set up using all kinds of bits and pieces. Clay or glass marbles were easily transportable, while fivestones or Jacks could always be substituted with pebbles if the proper toys weren't available.

Skipping, hopscotch, hide and seek, chasing games, dancing games, tag, catch, blindman's bluff, squeak piggy squeak and charades could also all be played in school playtime. Children of earlier generations needed to let off just as much steam as youngsters of today.

2. Favourite Playground Songs

ORANGES AND LEMONS

THESE are the games we all played and loved as children but which, sadly, are in danger of being forgotten as today's children play with the latest gadget or sit in front of the television instead of engaging in sociable games with their friends. Without these active games, today's children are losing the fight against obesity.

Ally Ally-O

Ally Ally-O means all the oceans and was used by sailors and their families as a cry for their return to their home port – across all the oceans. Some believe that the date, September 1st, denoted the day on which ships should be moored for the winter, although this is debatable. There is even one version which mentions the big ship sailing through the Manchester Ship Canal.

This is a game performed by a line of children with linked hands. The child at one end places their free hand against a wall. The child at the other end is a 'ship'. The ship leads the children in the chain right up to the far end where they pass through the arch made by the end child and the wall, and then, by going into a circle, under the second arch and so on. As the chain moves, each child gets turned the other way. As they weave, they sing

> Oh, the big ship sails on the ally ally-o
> The ally ally-o
> The ally ally-o
> The big ship sails on the ally ally-o
> On the first day of September.
> Oh, mother, father, may I go?
> May I go?
> May I go?
> Oh, mother, father, may I go?
> On the first day of September?

The Big Ship.

The Farmer's in the Dell

This classic game is played by a circle of children who have chosen one child to be the 'Farmer'. The Farmer stands in the centre of the circle while the others, holding hands, walk or skip while chanting the song. The Farmer chooses a Wife, who chooses a Child and so on. When the verse gets to the Dog, hopefully, there is a teacher, dinner lady or other adult playing. With great glee from the children, they are invariably the chosen victim, and are joyfully patted. Sometimes, if there are two adults, one is chosen as a bone, and the song slightly amended so everyone pats the bone as well as the dog – not logical, but a great way of slyly inflicting bodily harm on someone in authority...

The Farmer's in the Dell.

In some areas the song is known as The Farmer's In the Den, but in other respects it remains the same. Other variations include 'The dog wants a cat', 'The cat wants a rat' (or mouse), 'The mouse wants some cheese', etc, no doubt substituted by bruised teachers – although with child logic, it is still perfectly possible to pat the cheese. And the cat and rat, come to think of it!

There are regional differences for 'ee-i, ee-i' with some versions having 'derry-o', others 'adario', or Hey Ho the Dairy-o' and 'ee-i addio' in some northern parts of the UK. For some London-based children, 'ee-i, tiddly-i' is the nonsense line of choice.

My primary school in Welwyn Garden City boasted two special features – a wood and a dell, both of which were off limits except when the headmaster let us play there. To six and seven year olds, there was something very special, important and magical about singing this song in a real dell!

The farmer's in the dell
The farmer's in the dell
Ee-i, ee-i
The farmer's in the dell.

The farmer wants a wife
The farmer wants a wife
Ee-i, ee-i
The farmer wants a wife.

The wife wants a child
The wife wants a child
Ee-i, ee-i
The wife wants a child.

The child wants a nurse
The child wants a nurse
Ee-i, ee-i
The child wants a nurse.

The nurse wants a dog
The nurse wants a dog
Ee-i, ee-i
The nurse wants a dog.

The dog wants a bone
The dog wants a bone
Ee-i, ee-i
The dog wants a bone.

We all pat the dog
We all pat the dog
Ee-i, ee-i
We all pat the dog.

Cumulative chants

I remember playing The Farmer Wants A Wife where all the children form a big circle holding hands, with one person (the Farmer) in the middle and they choose a wife, then a baby, then a nurse etc until there are more and more children inside the circle and the others dance around them holding hands. As far as I can remember it was:

The farmer wants a wife,
The farmer wants a wife,
hey-ho-the-dairy-oh,

The farmer wants a wife, & so it goes on with:

The wife wants a child etc

The child wants a nurse etc

The nurse wants a dog etc

The dog wants a cat etc

The cat wants a mouse etc

The mouse wants some cheese etc

Then at the end

We all want some cheese,
We all want some cheese,
hey-ho-the-dairy-oh,
we all want some cheese...

Jayne Soule, treasure hunter! Loves collecting

In our version they all start leaving one by one until the cheese 'stands alone, Hi Ho the Dairy-oh, the cheese stands alone'.

Jill Jackson, animal lover, raised on fairytales

I think that the child wanted a nurse and then the nurse wanted a dog and the dog wanted a cat and the cat wanted a mouse...But it was a long time ago And I remember that the cheese at the end came in for a bit of rough treatment!

Jean Needle, age 64, librarian/administrator

Here We Go Gathering Nuts in May

A pretty song, not so common as it once was, and sung to the tune of Here We Go Round the Mulberry Bush. The concept of 'nuts in May' often puzzles people, as you expect it to be 'nuts in September'! In fact, originally the word was 'knots', another word for posies of flowers, or for the traditional grassy nosegays or knots worn to celebrate May Day. It is played by two lines of children. One row advance and then retreat, singing the first verse. The other row do the same singing the second verse. After the final verse, the two children named in the third and fifth verses must take hands and try to pull each other towards their row. The loser joins the winner's row and the game begins again.

Here we go gathering nuts in May,
Nuts in May, nuts in May.
Here we go gathering nuts in May,
On a cold and frosty morning.

Who will you have for nuts in May,
Nuts in May, nuts in May?
Who will you have for nuts in May,
On a cold and frosty morning.

We'll have (Anna) for nuts in May,
Nuts in May, nuts in May.
We'll have Anna for nuts in May,
On a cold and frosty morning.

Who will you send to fetch her away,
Fetch her away, fetch her away?
Who will you send to fetch her away,
On a cold and frosty morning?

We'll send (Jack) to fetch her away,
Fetch her away, fetch her away.
We'll send Jack to fetch her away,
On a cold and frosty morning.

Here We Go Round the Mulberry Bush

Another song beloved by youngsters, it combines movement, singing and plenty of vigorous actions. It is also a perfect song for improvisation. In Scandinavia, they 'go round the juniper bush' instead. One story goes that the rhyme may possibly have begun life as a chant by inmates of Wakefield prison, who regularly exercised around a mulberry bush which was in the prison yard. What words they sang, and whether they did all the actions is unknown! Apparently, a mulberry bush (actually a tree) can still be seen at the prison today

Chorus:

Here we go round the mulberry bush,
The mulberry bush, the mulberry bush.
Here we go round the mulberry bush,

On a cold and frosty morning.

This is the way we wash our clothes,
Wash our clothes, wash our clothes.
This is the way we wash our clothes,
On a cold and frosty morning.

Chorus:

This is the way we iron our clothes,
Iron our clothes, iron our clothes.
This is the way we iron our clothes,
On a cold and frosty morning.

Chorus:

This is the way we scrub the floor,
Scrub the floor, scrub the floor.
This is the way we scrub the floor,
On a cold and frosty morning.

Chorus:

This is the way we sweep the floor,
Sweep the house, sweep the floor.
This is the way we sweep the floor,
On a cold and frosty morning.

Chorus:

This is the way we polish the floor,
Sweep the house, polish the floor.
This is the way we polish the floor,
On a cold and frosty morning.

Chorus:

This is the way we mend our clothes,
Mend our clothes, mend our clothes.
This is the way we mend our clothes,
On a cold and frosty morning.

Chorus:

This is the way we bake our bread,
Bake our bread, bake our bread.
This is the way we bake our bread,
On a cold and frosty morning.

Chorus:

This is the way we go to church,
Go to church, go to church.
This is the way we go to church,

On a cold and frosty morning.

Here we go round the mulberry bush,
The mulberry bush, the mulberry bush.
Here we go round the mulberry bush,
On a cold and frosty morning.

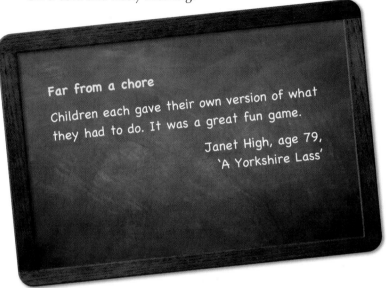

Far from a chore

Children each gave their own version of what
they had to do. It was a great fun game.

Janet High, age 79,
'A Yorkshire Lass'

When I was at infants and junior school, we sang this song a lot, but our version was more about personal care – whether this was something which had been drilled into us by the teachers, I don't know, but our playground version used to be (with verse six being sung particularly gleefully):

Chorus:

Here we go round the mulberry bush,
The mulberry bush, the mulberry bush.
Here we go round the mulberry bush,
On a cold and frosty morning.

This is the way we wash our hands,
Wash our hands, wash our hands.
This is the way we wash our hands,
On a cold and frosty morning.

Chorus:

This is the way we wash our face,
Wash our face, wash our face.
This is the way we wash our face,
On a cold and frosty morning.

Chorus:

This is the way we clean our teeth,
Clean our teeth, clean our teeth.
This is the way we clean our teeth,
On a cold and frosty morning.

Chorus:

This is the way we brush our hair,
Brush our hair, brush our hair.
This is the way we brush our hair,
On a cold and frosty morning.

Chorus:

This is the way we put on our vest,
Put on our vest, put on our vest.
This is the way we put on our vest,
On a cold and frosty morning.

Chorus:

This is the way we put on our knicks,
Put on our knicks, put on our knicks.
This is the way we put on our knicks,
On a cold and frosty morning.

Chorus:

This is the way we put on our dress,
Put on our dress, put on our dress.
This is the way we put on our dress,
On a cold and frosty morning.

Chorus:

This continued with coat, hat, scarf, gloves, socks, shoes before the final
verse:

Now we're ready to go for our walk,
Go for our walk, go for our walk.
Now we're ready to go for our walk,
On a cold and frosty morning.

Chorus:

I Sent a Letter

Another circle game is played by children seated in a ring. As they sing, one child runs around the outside carrying a hanky which she drops behind a seated child who takes it, secretly passing it to the next and so on. On the final 'you', the running child will tap her suspect on the shoulder who will produce the hanky. However, if the child has chosen wrongly, it is the turn of the child who actually has the hanky to be the runner

I sent a letter to my love
And on the way I dropped it.
One of you has picked it up
And put it in your pocket.
It wasn't you, It wasn't you, It wasn't you, It wasn't you,
It wasn't you, It wasn't you, It was YOU!

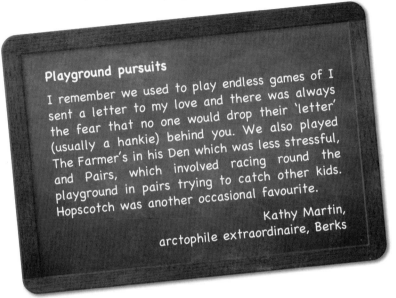

Playground pursuits

I remember we used to play endless games of I
sent a letter to my love and there was always
the fear that no one would drop their 'letter'
(usually a hankie) behind you. We also played
The Farmer's in his Den which was less stressful,
and Pairs, which involved racing round the
playground in pairs trying to catch other kids.
Hopscotch was another occasional favourite.

Kathy Martin,
arctophile extraordinaire, Berks

In and out the Dusty Bluebells

An old-fashioned, pretty game, still occasionally played today. It no doubt started
out as 'Dusky Bluebells' but as few children know that word, it soon became
Dusty. There is also a version where the children sing 'And who shall be my
partner' instead of 'I am your master'. The children link hands to form arches, and
stand in a circle. One child weaves in and out of the arches, pitta pattering with
their hands on the shoulders of the nearest child when the appropriate line of the
song is reached. Then the two of them join hands and weave in and out, and
another child joins them, and so on. Eventually, all the children end up weaving
in and out, and it can get quite complicated. When the leader pitta pats, the
following child pitta pats on the leader's shoulders, and as more children join the
weavers, a line forms of children each frantically pitta pattering on the shoulders
of the one in front of them!

In and out the dusty bluebells
In and out the dusty bluebells,
In and out the dusty bluebells
I am your master!
Pitta pitta patta on your shoulder
Pitta pitta patta on your shoulder,
Pitta pitta patta on your shoulder
I am your master!

In and out the Window

The children stand in a circle and hold hands, then begin to walk as they chant the rhyme. One version has one child in the middle, whose great moment comes in the penultimate verse when they can choose a sweetheart from the circling children. The 'sweetheart' joins the child in the ring. For the last verse the two children in the centre join hands and skip

In and out the window
In and out the window,
In and out the window
As we have gone before.
Round and round the levée
Round and round the levee,
Round and round the levée
As we have gone before.
Go and find your sweetheart
Go and find your sweetheart,
Go and find your sweetheart
As you have done before.
And now you'll both be happy
And now you'll both be happy,
And now you'll both be happy
As you have been before.

Many traditional games begin with a circle.

Window shopping

[In] our version of In and out the Windows ... children made a circle linking hands above their heads to form arches or windows. One person then went in one arch and out the next, round the circle. The rhyme was sung:

In and out the windows
In and out the windows,
In and out the windows
As you have done before.
Stand and face your playmate
Stand and face your playmate,
Stand and face your playmate
As you have done before.
Follow her to London
Follow her to London,
Follow her to London
As you have done before.

There were now two children going in and out the windows and this was continued until all the children formed a line with no windows left.

Janet High, age 79
'A Yorkshire Lass'

Kissing Game

A group of children stood in a circle, and one child went around as they sang

I gave, I gave her kisses one, kisses one
I gave, I gave her kisses one.
I gave her kisses one and she said - oh, do go on (at which point, one kiss is given)
So I went kissing kissing on.
I gave, I gave her kisses two, kisses two
I gave, I gave her kisses two,
I gave her kisses two and she said – that's one for you (two kisses to next child)
So I went kissing kissing on.

The verses were repeated as follows:

Kisses three – that's one for me
Kisses four – I want some more

Kisses five – oh, look alive
Kisses six – I'm in a fix
Kisses seven – oh, this is heaven
Kisses eight – now you'll be late
Kisses nine – oh, this is fine
Kisses ten – begin again

Early Twentieth Century postcard of London Bridge.

London Bridge is Falling Down

Similar to Oranges and Lemons, London Bridge is Falling Down has two children facing each other, their arms held high to form the arch of a bridge. The other children, holding on to each other, pass under the arch as they sing, and on the word 'Lady', the children forming the bridge drop their arms to catch the child. The child is either out, or, more usually, is allowed to choose one of the 'arches', standing behind them, holding onto their waist. When there are no more children to pass through the arch, a tug of war ensues.

The song dates back to the Sixteenth Century at least, and tells the history of London Bridge, which spans the River Thames. It has been added to over the centuries to show the development of the bridge and its raw materials such as iron and steel. The 'silver and gold' refers to the shops which lined the bridge in the Fourteenth Century. Another version, London Bridge is Broken Down is based on the rise and fall of Henry VIII's unpopular second wife, Anne Boleyn and depicts her as a 'gay Ladye'. In the better known version where the bridge falls down, 'The fair Lady' is reputed to be based either on Eleanor of Aquitaine (wife of Henry II whose reign saw London Bridge being rebuilt from 1176 in stone after a fire destroyed an earlier wooden bridge), or on the tradition of burying a virgin in the bridge to ensure its strength.

The bridge has been rebuilt several times after being destroyed in war (including by the Vikings in the Eleventh Century) and by fire or the sheer force of the mighty Thames. The stone bridge was an enormous achievement for its day and was the only stone bridge to cross the Thames until Westminster Bridge was opened in 1750.

As children rarely know all the words, they normally use only two or three of the most well-known verses

London Bridge is falling down
Falling down, falling down
London Bridge is falling down
My fair Lady.

Build it up with wood and clay
Wood and clay, wood and clay
Build it up with wood and clay
My fair Lady.

Wood and clay will wash away
Wash away, wash away
Wood and clay will wash away
My fair Lady.

Build it up with sticks and stones
Sticks and stones, sticks and stones
Build it up with sticks and stones
My fair Lady.

Sticks and stones will break away
Break away, break away
Sticks and stones will break away
My fair Lady.

Build it up with bricks and mortar
Bricks and mortar, bricks and mortar
Build it up with bricks and mortar
My fair Lady.

Bricks and mortar will not stay
Will not stay, will not stay
Bricks and mortar will not stay
My fair Lady.

Build it up with iron and steel
Iron and steel, iron and steel
Build it up with iron and steel
My fair Lady.

Iron and steel will bend and bow

Bend and bow, bend and bow
Iron and steel will bend and bow
My fair Lady.

Build it up with silver and gold
Silver and gold, silver and gold
Build it up with silver and gold
My fair Lady.

Silver and gold will be stolen away
Stolen away, stolen away
Silver and gold will be stolen away
My fair Lady.

Other verses include setting a man to keep watch at night, giving him a pipe to keep him awake and many other additions. Often, too, the following verse is tagged on at the end, presumably linked to the Anne Boleyn version:

Take the key and lock her up
Lock her up, lock her up
Take the key and lock her up
My fair Lady.

Falling down

The London Bridge game I played as a child had two children facing each other with their hands raised, to make a bridge, while other children went between. It ended with lyrics that went something like 'Take the keys and lock her up. My fair Lady'– at which time we would ensnare whichever child was going through our bridge at the time and sort of shake them up a bit!

Jill Jackson,
animal lover, raised on fairytales

Did you know?
London Bridge can be traced to Roman times, and was probably made of wood and clay as the rhyme says. It was constantly rebuilt or fortified. In the Twelfth Century, a stone bridge was erected, designed by a monk, Peter de Colechurch, and took 33 years to build. It featured 20 arches. This bridge survived the Great Fire of London in 1666, though was weakened. In the 1820s a new London Bridge was built, but on a different site, to the north of the old one. When another new London Bridge was built, in the 1960s, the 1820s bridge was transported to Arizona, USA, stone by stone.

Forming an arch.

I remember playing this game. Two children would join hands and raise their arms to form the arch of the bridge, but first they would have walked away from the group to decide which would be 'silver' and which 'gold'. Then they formed the arch and the other children passed under the arch in single file all singing, 'London Bridge is falling down, falling down, falling down. London Bridge is falling down, my fair Lady'. When they reached 'My fair lady', the two children lowered their arms on either side of whoever was in between them.

Then the two children swayed back and forth so that their 'prisoner' actually stepped forward and backward within their arms, and they all continued in sing-song, 'Take the key and lock her up, lock her up, lock her up. Take the key and lock her up, my fair Lady'. Then the 'prisoner' was walked forward a bit and asked, "Do you want to pay with silver or gold?" The prisoner whispered her answer so none of the children in the line could hear it. If the prisoner said silver she took the place of the child forming the bridge who had chosen to be silver, and the same with the gold. The child who was silver then joined the line. When new children formed the bridge they decided which would be silver and which gold and the game continued.

There were many verses to this rhyme, I am thinking now that we used one about 'Gold and silver have I none, have I none, have I none. Gold and silver have I none, my fair lady', and then we asked how the captured child would pay. Sometimes, when the two children forming the bridge did the swaying sideways movements more quickly, the 'prisoner' could get her feet tangled trying to keep up with their movements. I was among the smallest in my class and this often happened to me, particularly if the 'bridge' was much taller, with a longer reach. I took more steps to their sway!

Jo Birch, age 72.
Enjoys life to the full

London's Burning

A classic song with plenty of fun actions, it's based on the Great Fire of London (1666) but written much later – there were no fire engines then although a fire service, of sorts, had been around in Roman times. This song would have had added meaning for schoolchildren during the Blitz when London burnt again

London's Burning! London's Burning!
Fetch the engines, fetch the engines!
Fire, fire! Fire, fire!
Pour on water, pour on water!

Lucy Locket

This is quite an old rhyme, dating back at least two centuries. Several ladies called Kitty Fisher have made their mark in history. One is a beauty, of 'negligent virtue' who was painted by Reynolds in the 1700s. Her portrait hangs in Petworth House. This is a similar game to I Sent a Letter

> *Lucy Locket lost her pocket*
> *Kitty Fisher found it,*
> *But there wasn't any in it*
> *But a ribbon round it.*

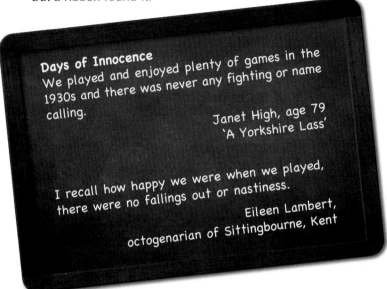

Days of Innocence
We played and enjoyed plenty of games in the 1930s and there was never any fighting or name calling.

Janet High, age 79
'A Yorkshire Lass'

I recall how happy we were when we played, there were no fallings out or nastiness.

Eileen Lambert,
octogenarian of Sittingbourne, Kent

Old Roger is Dead

This is an action game, which begins with a circle of children and one child lying in the middle of the circle (Old Roger). This is a variation of the song Oliver Cromwell Lay Buried and Dead. Both songs involve a lot of playacting

> *Old Roger is dead and lies in his grave,*
> *Lies in his grave*
> *Lies in his grave.*
> *Old Roger is dead and lies in his grave*
> *Ee, ay, lies in his grave.*
> *(The children point at Roger)*
>
> *There grew an old apple tree over his head,*
> *Over his head*
> *Over his head.*
> *There grew an old apple tree over his head*
> *Ee, ay, over his head.*
> *(The children wave their arms like trees)*
>
> *The apples grew ripe and they all dropped off,*

All dropped off
All dropped off.
The apples grew ripe and they all dropped off
Ee, ay all dropped off.
(Children simulate apples dropping off with arm movements –
sometimes balls are used to throw at Roger!)

There came an old woman a-picking them up
Picking them up
Picking them up.
There came an old woman a-picking them up
Ee, ay, picking them up.
(One child walks around the inside of the circle, holding up her skirt
with one hand as she pretends to fill it with apples.)

Old Roger got up and he gave her a thump
Gave her a thump
Gave her a thump.
Old Roger got up and he gave her a thump
Ee, ay, gave her a thump.
(Old Roger thumps the old lady!)

This made the old woman go hippity hop
Hippity hop
Hippity hop.
This made the old woman go hippity hop
Ee, ay, hippity hop.

(The old woman pretends to be lame and stumbles around the circle – the
next person she touches is the new 'Old Roger', and the game begins again).

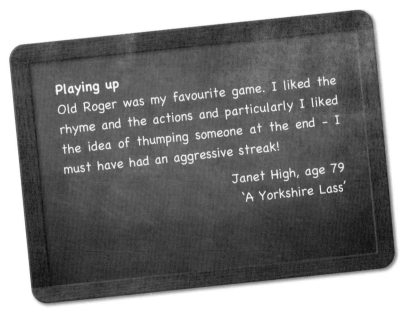

Playing up
Old Roger was my favourite game. I liked the rhyme and the actions and particularly I liked the idea of thumping someone at the end – I must have had an aggressive streak!

Janet High, age 79
'A Yorkshire Lass'

Oliver Cromwell Lay Buried and Dead

This classic song refers to the overthrow of the Lord Protector and the Restoration of the monarchy in 1660. As Cromwell was a Puritan, the idea of him giving the 'old woman' a drink was intended as an insult but the idea and actions always fill children with glee. The last line is always delivered as a challenging shout

Oliver Cromwell lay buried and dead,
Hee-haw, buried and dead,
There grew an old apple-tree over his head,
Hee-haw, over his head.
The apples were ripe and ready to fall,
Hee-haw, ready to fall,
There came an old woman to gather them all,
Hee-haw, gather them all.
Oliver rose and gave her a drop,
Hee-haw, gave her a drop,
Which made the old woman go hippity hop,
Hee-haw, hippity hop.
The saddle and bridle, they lie on the shelf,
Hee-haw, lie on the shelf,
If you want any more you can sing it yourself,
Hee-haw, sing it yourself.

On the Mountain

Children form a circle, with one child ('The lady') in the middle. They skip round her as they sing. When they sing 'a nice young man', she chooses someone, and holding hands, they skip around the inside of the circle, while the outer group also skip, repeating the song

On the mountain
Stands a lady,
Who she is
I do not know.
All she wants is
Gold and silver,
All she wants is
A nice young beau.
Madam, will you walk?
Madam, will you talk?
Madam, will you marry me?
No!
Not if I buy you the keys of Heaven?
Not if I buy you a coach and chair?
Not if I buy you a comb of silver
To place in your bonny, bonny hair?
No!

Oranges and Lemons

Another very familiar game is Oranges and Lemons, which was one of those playground games usually initiated by bored dinner ladies who wanted to snatch a few minutes respite. Oranges and Lemons has a centuries' old history, based on the bells of London, and dates back to a Square Dance of that name in 1665. It's often grouped with nursery rhymes, but is also a game in its own right.

The rhyme has a sinister history, based around the bells of the City of London which heralded morning executions. St Sepulchre-without-Newgate was opposite the Old Bailey (the Bells of Old Bailey) and, until 1783, were used to time the executions, then being replaced by Newgate's own bell when the Tyburn gallows moved from what's now Marble Arch to where the current Old Bailey stands. This helps date the song as pre-1783 when the tenor bell of St Sepulchre no longer called in the morning hangings.

The last few lines were added much later and refer to the gallows and the axe of executions. The candle is believed to be the one used by the Bellman of St Sepulchre who would ring a large hand bell, known as the Execution Bell, at midnight outside the prisoner's cell, prior to the day of execution.

The game is played by choosing two children – who secretly agree which of them is an orange and which will be a lemon – to form an arch by linking their hands, and the rest of the children pass underneath. When the verse reaches the Chop, Chop, Chop, the hands are lowered. The child that is 'dead' must whisper whether they choose to be an orange or a lemon and stand behind that person, with their arms around that waist. When all the children have been caught, a tug of war ensues between the opposing sides.

Oranges and Lemons has been enjoyed by children for centuries. This postcard dates from 1908.

39

The City of London churches mentioned are:

- St Clement Eastcheap or St Clement Danes - Opinions vary but the bells of St Clement Danes now ring out the popular tune.
- St Martin Ongar - The words commemorating Newgate's time as a debtor's prison.
- St Sepulchre-without-Newgate - Opposite the Old Bailey, hence the Bells of Old Bailey.
- St Leonard's Shoreditch - Where many Tudor actors, including Richard Burbage and Richard Tarlton are buried.
- St Dunstan's, Stepney - Its nickname is the Church of the High Seas because of its link to the sea and sailors. There are 10 bells in the belfry.
- St Mary-le-Bow - True Cockneys are said to have been born within sound of these famous bells - there are more bells than just the Great Bell of St Mary-le-Bow mentioned in the rhyme.

The words tend to vary, but one of the most commonly found versions is:

Oranges and Lemons
Say the Bells of St Clement's,
You owe me five farthings
Say the Bells of St Martin's.
When will you pay me?
Say the Bells of Old Bailey,
When I grow rich
Say the Bells of Shoreditch.
When will that be?
Say the Bells of Stepney,
I do not know
Says the Great Bell of Bow.
Here comes a candle to light you to bed
And here comes a chopper to chop off your head
Chop, Chop, Chop,
The last man's dead!

Poor Jenny is A-weeping

Songs such as Poor Jenny is A-weeping, In and out the Dusty Bluebells and I Sent a Letter, though often seen as party games or 'organised' games initiated by the teacher, were certainly played in 1950s and 1960s playgrounds, started by the children themselves.

Jenny knelt with her hands to her face, 'weeping', while the other children held hands to form a circle and walked around her as they sang. On the next verse, she stood up to choose a 'Sweetheart'. The final verse had the children all skipping around

> Poor Jenny is a-weeping, a-weeping, a-weeping,
> Poor Jenny is a-weeping
> On a bright sunny day.
> Stand up and choose your loved one, your loved one, your loved one,
> Stand up and choose your loved one
> On a bright sunny day.
> And now she is so happy, so happy, so happy,
> And now she is so happy
> On a bright sunny day.

Poor Mary

Played in a similar way to Poor Jenny is A-weeping, Mary (in the centre of the ring) acts out the song, choosing another child on the line 'And choose the one you love so sweet'. They join hands and walk or skip in the centre of the ring, going in the opposite direction to the children in the outer circle, who sing the last few lines. Then a new Mary is chosen, often the other child in the centre, Mary's 'chosen' one

> Poor Mary sat a-weeping, a-weeping, a-weeping,
> Poor Mary sat a-weeping on a bright summer's day.
> On this carpet she shall kneel
> Till the grass grows in the field,
> Stand up, stand up upon your feet
> And choose the one you love so sweet.
> Now you are married, you must be good
> And help your wife to chop the wood
> Chop, chop, chop.

Ring-a-ring-o'-roses

Younger children are especially fond of Ring-a-ring-o'-roses, though by the time children reach the grand old age of six, it has definitely been relegated to the sidelines. This is another of those rhymes with sinister overtones, though this may, in fact, be based more on folklore than reality. However, it is certainly intriguing to think that such a delightful song might refer to the symptoms of the bubonic plague of 1665. One of the plague's first symptoms was a distinctive rosy rash, another was violent sneezing. Pockets would contain posies of sweet-smelling herbs to counteract bad smells (it was believed bad smells spread the disease). The 'all fall down', of course, was the person dying.

Children form a circle and skip around as they chant the words. On singing 'We all fall down' everyone does just that! It's worth pointing out that small children bounce much more readily than older ones, which is another reason why it's regarded as an infant's game. Also, it is somewhat undignified!

> *Ring-a-ring-o'-roses*
> *A pocket full of posies*
> *A-tishoo, A-tishoo*
> *We all fall down.*

Another, later verse, perhaps added to make the game more complete, is:

> *The cows are in the meadow*
> *Eating buttercups*
> *A-tishoo, A-tishoo!*
> *We all jump up.*

Other verses include:

> *The King has sent his daughter*
> *To fetch a pail of water*
> *A-tishoo, A-tishoo*
> *We all fall down.*

> *The bird upon the steeple*
> *Sits high above the people*
> *A-tishoo, A-tishoo*
> *We all fall down.*

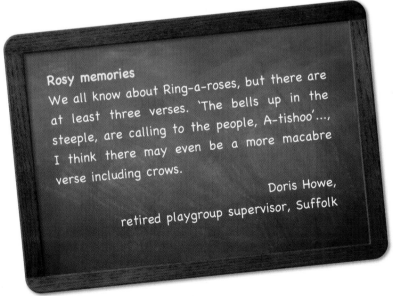

Rosy memories

We all know about Ring-a-roses, but there are at least three verses. 'The bells up in the steeple, are calling to the people, A-tishoo'..., I think there may even be a more macabre verse including crows.

Doris Howe,
retired playgroup supervisor, Suffolk

3. Sing Song Chants

WITH A KNICK-KNACK PADDYWHACK

THERE are thousands of songs which can be sung with actions - not games in themselves, purely an enjoyable way of passing a few minutes while sitting in the playground, or maybe in the queue, waiting to go back into school or for 'second sitting' at dinner time. Amongst the favourites are This Old Man, One Man Went To Mow, Baby Bumblebee and Ten Green Bottles. Another great favourite, certainly in the early-1960s, was With My Hand, though teachers rather disapproved of this, several telling us it was 'too common'!

Baby Bumblebee

I'm bringing home a baby bumblebee,
Won't my mummy be so proud of me.
(Child cups hands together as if holding a bee)

I'm bringing home a baby bumblebee,
Ouch! It stung me!
(Shake hands as if been stung)

I'm squashing up the baby bumblebee,
Won't my mummy be so proud of me.
('Squash' the bee between palms of hands)

I'm squashing up a baby bumblebee,
Ugh! It's yucky!
(Opens hands to look at mess)

I'm wiping off the baby bumblebee,
Won't my mummy be so proud of me.
(Wipes hands on clothes)

I'm wiping off the baby bumblebee,
Now my mummy won't be mad at me!
(Holds up hands to show they're now clean)

Bee song
We often used to sing this in the playground. it was fun to do, especially the squashing up bit!

Jenna Brewer,
born 1980, ballet and bunny enthusiast

One Man Went to Mow

This cumulative playground classic can carry on indefinitely but generally stops at ten men. The actions include holding up the correct number of fingers, pushing an imaginary mower and patting the dog, Spot. Sometimes, the dog's name, Spot, is omitted but children often shout 'woof' after the word Spot.

One man went to mow
Went to mow a meadow
One man and his dog, Spot
Went to mow a meadow.

Two men went to mow
Went to mow a meadow
Two men, one man and his dog, Spot,
Went to mow a meadow.

Three men went to mow
Went to mow a meadow
Three men, two men, one man and his dog, Spot,
Went to mow a meadow.

Ten Green Bottles

A classic which can involve hundreds of green bottles on particularly long car journeys or can be limited to just 10 at break time. The song continues until there are none left. Sometimes, the last line of the verse when only one bottle is left, is sung gleefully as 'There'll be nothing but the smell left hanging on the wall!' accompanied by much holding of noses. Actions normally consist of holding up fingers for the number of bottles and clapping on the word 'fall'

Ten green bottles hanging on the wall
Ten green bottles hanging on the wall
And if one green bottle should accidentally fall,
There'll be nine green bottles hanging on the wall.

Nine green bottles hanging on the wall
Nine green bottles hanging on the wall
And if one green bottle should accidentally fall,
There'll be eight green bottles hanging on the wall.

Eight green bottles hanging on the wall
Eight green bottles hanging on the wall
And if one green bottle should accidentally fall,
There'll be seven green bottles hanging on the wall.

This Old Man

Also known as the children's marching song, there are many different ways of performing the actions; in one version the appropriate number of fingers are held up when the number is sung. The words 'knick-knack' are accompanied by claps, 'paddywack' is drummed on any nearby object and 'rolling home' is accompanied by circular hand movements

This old man
He played one
He played knick-knack on my drum
With a knick-knack paddywack, give a dog a bone
This old man went rolling home.

This old man
He played two
He played knick-knack on my shoe
With a knick-knack paddywack, give a dog a bone
This old man went rolling home.

This old man
He played three
He played knick-knack on my knee
With a knick-knack paddywack, give a dog a bone
This old man went rolling home.

This old man
He played four
He played knick-knack on my door
With a knick-knack paddywack, give a dog a bone
This old man went rolling home.

This old man
He played five
He played knick-knack on my hive
With a knick-knack paddywack, give a dog a bone
This old man went rolling home.

This old man
He played six
He played knick-knack on my sticks
With a knick-knack paddywack, give a dog a bone
This old man went rolling home.

This old man
He played seven
He played knick-knack on my heaven
With a knick-knack paddywack, give a dog a bone
This old man went rolling home.

This old man
He played eight

He played knick-knack on my gate
With a knick-knack paddywack, give a dog a bone
This old man went rolling home.

This old man
He played nine
He played knick-knack on my line
With a knick-knack paddywack, give a dog a bone
This old man went rolling home.

This old man
He played ten
He played knick-knack on my hen
With a knick-knack paddywack, give a dog a bone
This old man went rolling home.

With My Hand

The song which many of my teachers dismissed as being 'too common' – surely an incentive to sing it at playtime! Actions include touching the top of the head on the first line, then touching the appropriate parts of the anatomy as they are reached. Obviously, this song lends itself to plenty of gleeful additions! Sometimes, the last line of the verse is sung as 'When I was at school'

With my hand on myself
What do I hear?
This is my brainboxer
I do declare
Brainboxer and knicky knacky noo
That's what they teach us
At (insert school's name) school

With my hand on myself
What do I hear?
These are my eye-peepers
I do declare
Brainboxer, eye-peepers and knicky knacky noo
That's what they teach us
At (insert school's name) school

With my hand on myself
What do I hear?
This is my nose-wiper
I do declare
Brainboxer, eye-peepers, nose-wiper and knicky knacky noo
That's what they teach us
At (insert school's name) school

And so on, continuing with cake eater, chin chopper, chest protector, breadbasket, knee-knocker and foot-stomper.

47

SONG PARODIES

Topical tunes

Sung to the tune of Catch a Falling Star, this rhyme celebrated the launch of the Soviet Union's unmanned satellites, the Sputnik series, in October, 1957

Catch a falling Sputnik
Put it in a matchbox
Never let it fade away.
Catch a falling Sputnik
Put it in a matchbox
Send it to the USA.

Western wonders

Sung to the tune of The Yellow Rose of Texas, this mid-1950s song celebrates the legendary hero who was portrayed in the 1954 film, Davy Crockett, King of the Wild Frontier. Initially a 1955 film called The Man from Laramie, Laramie became a popular TV series. The enduring popularity of the American West can be seen in this silly playground song

The Yellow Rose of Texas
And the man from Laramie
Went to Davy Crockett's to have a cup of tea.
The tea was so delicious
They had another cup
And then poor Davy Crockett
Had to do the washing up.

The Yellow Rose of Texas
And the Man From Laramie
Went to Davy Crockett's to have a cup of tea.
The tea they didn't like it
They poured it down the drain
And then poor Davy Crockett
Had to lick it up again.

Cheeky children

Sung to the tune of the classic Welsh melody, The Ash Grove, this would have been hugely appealing

My teacher's a funny'un
With a nose like a pickled onion
A face liked a squashed tomato
And legs like matchsticks.

The song below was sung to the tune of Clementine and was especially popular around Bonfire Night

> *Build a bonfire, build a bonfire*
> *Put the teachers on the top*
> *Put (headmaster's name) in the middle*
> *And we'll burn the blooming lot!*

Batman smells

Sung to the tune of Jingle Bells, this celebrates the popular TV series starring Adam West as Batman/Bruce Wayne and Burt Ward as Robin/Dick Grayson

> *Jingle bells, Batman smells*
> *Robin laid an egg*
> *The Batmobile lost a wheel*
> *And the Joker lost a leg.*
> *Jingle bells, Batman smells*
> *Robin flew away*
> *The Batmobile lost a wheel*
> *And the Joker said hooray.*

Wartime humour

Snow White and the Seven Dwarfs (1937) was Disney's first full-length production. Using the tune of one of the most popular songs from the pre-war film, this wartime parody mocks Hitler, providing much needed light-relief during the days of evacuation and bombing

> *Whistle while you work*
> *Hitler is a jerk*
> *He is barmy*
> *So's his army*
> *Whistle while you work.*

Popular culture at Christmas

Sung to the tune of We Three Kings, this 1960s parody celebrates popular culture – scooters and the Beatles

> *We three kings of Orient are*
> *One in a taxi*
> *One in a car,*
> *One on a scooter*
> *Tooting his hooter*
> *Following yonder star.*

> *We three Beatles of Liverpool are*
> *John on a bike*
> *Paul in a car,*

George on a scooter
Pressing the hooter
Following Ringo Starr.

Sung to the tune of While Shepherds Watched, this irreverent song is a Christmas favourite

While Shepherds washed their socks by night,
All seated round the tub,
A bar of sunlight soap came down,
And they began to scrub.

Christmas carols were turned into mischievous playground verse.

50

4. Rhymes and Puns

ONE POTATO, TWO POTATO

BEFORE a game could start, it was necessary to decide who was to be the leader, It, the turners of the rope, or the one who first threw or kicked the ball. Children tended to be scrupulously fair over whose turn it was, and who went first, and dipping rhymes were taken seriously, an integral part of the ritual. They still are, of course. Sometimes, the rhymes were so long, or involved, that

Who's IT?

they took up most of playtime, leaving no time to actually play the game. But it was all part of the fun!

There are hundreds of dipping rhymes, and dozens of regional variations; invariably they are performed by one child who points to their neighbours in turn (and themself) as they dip. Of course, the most difficult thing is to decide which child will perform the dipping rhyme...!

Additionally, there are many other kinds of rhymes, from put-downs used to tease or annoy other children, to general parodies of songs, or jingles and nonsense verse, all designed to amuse. There are also the fortune-telling rhymes, beloved by children counting anything from buttons on a cardigan to pebbles found in the playground.

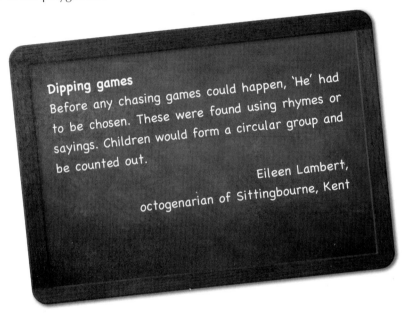

Dipping games
Before any chasing games could happen, 'He' had to be chosen. These were found using rhymes or sayings. Children would form a circular group and be counted out.

Eileen Lambert,
octogenarian of Sittingbourne, Kent

Counting and Dipping Games
These often silly songs would be used to determine who was out until only It remained. They were known as counting or dipping rhymes.

Apple Pudding, Apple Pie
Other endings for this rhyme depended on which colour the 'victim' chose

> *Apple Pudding, Apple Pie*
> *Did you ever tell a lie?*
> *No!*
> *Yes you did, you broke your mother's teapot*
> *What colour was it?*
> *Blue*
> *No, it wasn't, it was gold*
> *That's another lie you told!*

No, it wasn't, it was red
That's another lie you said!

No, it wasn't, it was blue
Nothing that you said was true!

No, it wasn't, it was white
Nothing that you said was right!

Bye Baby Bunting

Bye baby bunting
Daddy's gone a-hunting
He's gone to get a rabbit skin
To wrap the baby bunting in
Bye baby bunting.

Counting sheep

Another form of counting or dipping rhyme, which varies from school to school and generation to generation, is said to be based on the so-called 'shepherds' score', a method used by shepherds counting their sheep

Yan, Tan, Tethera, Methera, Pimp,
Othera, Lethera, Hothera, Dothera, Dick.

Which, in turn, brings to mind a nursery rhyme, which is occasionally used for counting out, and which might well have been based on the shepherds' score:

Hickory Dickory Dock
The mouse ran up the clock
The clock struck one
The mouse ran down
Hickory, Dickory, Dock

Dip Dip Dip

Dip Dip Dip
My little ship
Sailed on the water
Like a cup and saucer
O - U - T spells OUT!

Eenie Meanie

This next rhyme, beginning Eenie, Meanie, Mackeracker, appears countrywide with dozens of variations

I went to a Chinese laundry
To buy a loaf of bread.
They wrapped it up in a tablecloth
And this is what they said:
Eenie, meanie mackeracker
Eer I dominacker

Chickeracker, lollypopper
Om pom push.
Eeenie, meanie mackeracker
Ere I dominacker
Sugar packer lollipoppa
Om dom push.

(Also, see chapter nine – Clapping Games).

A popular rhyme which is said to date from the 1850s. There are several different versions of this, not all fit to be printed nowadays

Eeenie meanie minie moe
Catch a baby by the toe
If it squeals let it go,
Eeenie meanie minie moe.

Eeenie meanie minie moe
Catch a tiger by his toe
If he hollers let him go
Eeenie meanie minie moe.

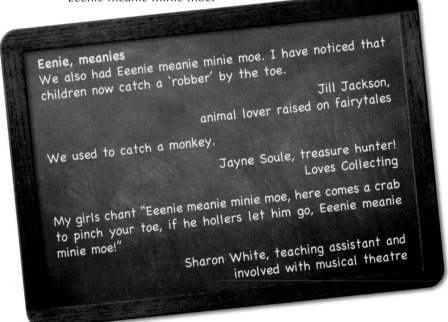

Eenie, meanies
We also had Eeenie meanie minie moe. I have noticed that children now catch a 'robber' by the toe.

Jill Jackson,
animal lover raised on fairytales

We used to catch a monkey.

Jayne Soule, treasure hunter!
Loves Collecting

My girls chant "Eeenie meanie minie moe, here comes a crab to pinch your toe, if he hollers let him go, Eeenie meanie minie moe!"

Sharon White, teaching assistant and involved with musical theatre

Have a Cigarette, Sir

Have a cigarette, sir
No, sir.
Why, sir?
'Cos I've got a cough, sir!
Let me hear you cough, sir?
(Coughs)
Very bad indeed sir

Ought to be in bed sir
O - U - T spells out!

Higgledy Piggledy
One school of thought suggests this next rhyme is based on an older one about a lady of a certain reputation, called Little Blue Betty, and which includes the lines 'Gentlemen came every day...she hopped upstairs to make her bed'

Higgledy Piggledy
My black hen
She lays eggs
For gentlemen
Sometimes nine
And sometimes ten
Higgledy Piggledy
My black hen.

Higgedy, piggedy,
I celiggedy,
Pomperary jig
Every man that has no hair
Ought to wear a wig
So - higgedy, piggedy,
I celiggedy,
Pomperary jig.

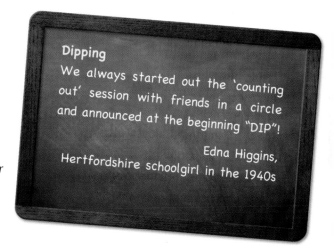

Dipping

We always started out the 'counting out' session with friends in a circle and announced at the beginning "DIP"!

Edna Higgins,
Hertfordshire schoolgirl in the 1940s

Ink Pink Pen Stink
This would be performed by the children standing in a circle and pointing at each one in turn with each word. The child who is pointed at on the word 'stink' is out

Inky Pinky Ponky

Inky pinky ponky
Daddy bought a donkey
Donkey died
Daddy cried
Inky Pinky Ponky.

My Bonnie Lies over the Ocean
A popular Scottish folk song believed to be based on the story of Bonnie Prince Charlie who fled over the ocean to France when his rebellion failed. The song had many variations, including one recorded by Tony Sheridan with the little-known Beatles as a backing combo (credited as the Beat Brothers), and several comical versions. The Bunny parody below dates from a 1948 Bugs Bunny film

My bonnie lies over the ocean
My bonnie lies over the sea,
My bonnie lies over the ocean
Oh, bring back my bonnie to me.

My bunny lies over the ocean
My bunny lies over the sea,
My bunny lies over the ocean
Oh, let's have a nice cup of tea.

Nonsense words

Nonsense rhymes based on sounds like Ip Dip are typical 'dipping' games to choose who's It

Ip dip
Sky's blue
Who's it?
Not you
Not because you're dirty
Not because you're clean
My mum says you're the fairy
queen
O-U-T spells out!

Ip dip doo
Cat's got the flu
Dog's got the chicken pox
Out go you.

Ippa dippa dation
My operation
How many people
Are waiting at the station?

Dip a penn'orth of chips
To grease your rosy lips
Out goes you.

The next is a spoof rhyme from the cult TV programme *Red Dwarf*

Ippy dippy
My space shippy
On a course so true
Past Neptune and Pluto's moon
The one I choose is you.

Iggy oggy
Black froggy
Iggy oggy out!

Ickle ockle
Blue bottle
Fishes in the sea
If you want a pretty girl
Please choose me!

Sing song

Many counting out games used nursery rhymes such as Bye Baby Bunting, or current popular songs such as My Bonnie Lies over the Ocean.

Eileen Lambert,
octogenarian,
Sittingbourne, Kent

Ibble obble
Black bobble
Ibble obble out!
Turn a dirty dishcloth
Inside out
Once if it's dirty
Twice if it's clean
Ibble obble
Black bobble
Ibble obble
Out!

Once I Caught a Fish Alive

This popular rhyme is believed to have been based on an Eighteenth Century rhyme and is sung with finger wiggling actions

One, two, three, four, five
Once I caught a fish alive.
Six, seven, eight, nine, ten
Then I let it go again.
Why did you let it go?
Because it bit my finger so.
Which finger did it bite?
This little finger on the right.

One Potato, Two Potato

This classic rhyme was carried out using clenched fists, and when the chanter got to 'more', the person whose fist the chanter's fist had reached, put it behind their backs. When both fists were behind their backs, a person was out. Finally, It would be the last person with a fist still in play

One potato, two potato
Three potato, four,
Five potato, six potato,
Seven potato, more.

A variation was:

One potato, two potatoes,
Three potatoes, four.
Four potatoes, five potatoes,
Who wants more?

One Potato.

Spud u like

We used to do "One potato, two potato, three potato, four - five potato, six potato, seven potato more." This was done in a circle with everyone having their fists in front of them while one person touched each fist in turn (as a potato). Whoever was touched on the seventh potato had to put that fist behind them. Then they would go around again. Each time the seventh potato (fist) was touched, that child would have to put that fist behind them. First one to have both fists behind them was It.

Jill Jackson,
animal lover, raised on fairytales

There was a rhyme with rounded hands
'One potato two potato three potato four
Five potato, six potato seven potato more'

Very weird.....

Doris Howe,
retired playgroup supervisor, Suffolk

Two Potato.

One Two

One Two
Sky Blue
Who's Out?
Not You!

One, Two, Three

One, two, three,
Mother caught a flea
She put it in the teapot
To make a cup of tea.
When the tea was ready
the flea began to hop
And when she put the water
in the flea went pop.

Two, four, six, eight
Mary at the cottage gate
Eating cherries off a plate
Two, four, six, eight.

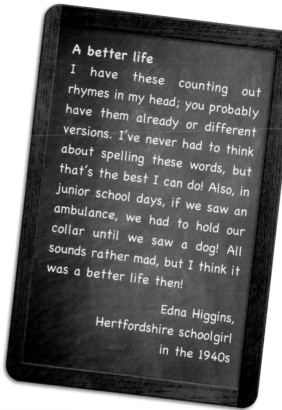

A better life

I have these counting out rhymes in my head; you probably have them already or different versions. I've never had to think about spelling these words, but that's the best I can do! Also, in junior school days, if we saw an ambulance, we had to hold our collar until we saw a dog! All sounds rather mad, but I think it was a better life then!

Edna Higgins,
Hertfordshire schoolgirl
in the 1940s

Rock, Paper, Scissors

Another way of choosing who would be It was to play Rock, Paper, Scissors (players put one hand behind their backs, then at a given signal (often Ching Chang Cholla) showed the hand as either flat (paper), two fingers (scissors) or clenched fist for rock or stone

Scissors cut paper
Rock crushes scissors
Paper wraps rock

Time for counting

One-o-clock,
Two-o-clock,
Three-o-clock,
Four
Five-o-clock,
Six-o-clock,
Seven-o-clock,
More.

NONSENSE VERSES AND FORTUNE TELLING

Fortune telling for girls

The words would be sung or chanted as the girls counted cardigan buttons, prune or cherry stones to tell their fortunes. The tinker tailor part of the game is the best-known part of it and has several variations. The game has influenced John le Carré (Tinker, Tailor, Soldier, Spy), bands including Queen and Supertramp and even *Star Trek* which had an episode entitled 'Tinker, Tenor, Doctor, Spy'

When shall I marry?
This year
Next year
Sometime
Never?

What will he be?
Tinker
Tailor
Soldier
Sailor
Rich man
Poor man
Beggar man
Thief.

What shall I be?
Lady
Baby
Gipsy
Queen

What shall I wear?
Silk
Satin
Cotton
Rags?

How shall I get my wedding clothes?
Given
Borrowed
Bought
Stolen?

How shall I get to the church?
Coach
Carriage
Wheelbarrow
Dung cart?

Future husbands?

Ours was 'tinker, tailor, cowboy, sailor, rich man, poor man, beggar man, thief, doctor, lawyer, merchant chief'.
[Note, this version comes from an Ellery Queen Novel, 'Double, Double' (also known as 'The Case of the Seven Murders'), from 1949]

Jill Jackson, animal lover, raised on fairytales

We used to say 'tinker, tailor, soldier, sailor, rich man, poor man, beggar man, thief' with a dessert that had cherry, plum or any fruit with a stone in, to see who you were going to marry – if you had four stones you were going to marry a sailor etc., I also seem to remember another one with fruit stones relating to what you would wear on your wedding day – silk, satin, cotton but I can't remember the rest.

Margaret Follwell, doll, bear and toy collector, Wiltshire

We said 'tinker, tailor, soldier, sailor, rich man, poor man, beggar man, thief', but it was to pick the first in a game. Of course this was World War II, so 'soldier, sailor...' was the way to say it, although my sons in the 1950s said the same.

Jo Birch, age 72, enjoys life to the full

Where will we live?
House
Cottage
Bungalow
Pigsty?

Grandma's Pussycat

Rat-a-tat-tat
Who is that?
Only grandma's pussycat.
What do you want?
A pint of milk
Where's your money?
In my pocket
Where's your pocket?
I forgot it
Oh, you silly pussycat!

Knickers on the Line!

What's the time?
Half past nine
Hang your knickers on the line.
When a policeman comes along
Take them off and put them on!

Michael Finnegan

This next rhyme was a favourite at the junior school in Welwyn Garden City which I attended, because we had a very popular teacher called Michael Guinery

There was an old man
Called Michael Finnegan
He grew whiskers on his chinnegan
The wind came out and blew them in again
Poor old Michael Finnegan
Begin Again!

We usually altered it to:

There was an old man
Called Michael Guinery
He grew whiskers on his chinery
The wind came out and blew them inery
Poor old Michael Guinery
Beginery!

Piggy on the Railway

Piggy on the railway
Picking up stones.
Along came an engine
And broke piggy's bones
"Hey," said piggy
"That's not fair!"
"Oh", said the engine driver
"I don't care!"

Pincha, Puncha

I played this at primary school during the 1950s. A short line of children would form, and they would advance across the playground, encircling any child in their path as they chanted.

The majority of their victims, unwilling to suffer a group pinching or punching session (however gentle it might be), and loathe to reveal if they were 'sweet' on anyone, took the easy option of joining in the ring. Gradually, the ring would get bigger and bigger, until eventually there might be a hundred or so children linking hands, and they ran out of victims

Pincha, puncha, join in the ring
Or tell me your sweetheart's name.

5. Games Without Props

SIMON SAYS, "WHO NEEDS A PLAYSTATION?"

MANY games don't need chants, rhymes, jingles or any kind of prop. Often, these are the spontaneous kinds, triggered by a tap on the shoulder resulting in a full scale chase, a quick discussion – 'let's play Sticky Toffee', an impetuous handstand, or maybe a 'bet you can't find me if I hide' remark. Some of the games here are traditional, some are new, but all of them are likely to vary across the country, because the glorious thing about children is that they are all individuals wanting to make their mark on a game.

In the 1960s, we would spend many happy summer playtimes practising handstands on the school field – it was a softer landing than on the asphalt playground. We loved our school field; by the age of 13 or 14, games were, on the whole, beneath us, apart from I Spy or various guessing, clapping routines. Lunch

Forming an orderly queue - very British!

breaks were spent sitting near the edge of the field where the grass was longer, and we would lie back and watch the skylarks as they soared into the blue sky, pouring out their songs. Once, one of the girls heard faint squeaking and discovered a nest of field mice, so we quietly crept away in the hope we hadn't disturbed the mother. We would laugh and gossip and exchange confidences, and we all looked so neat in our pale blue cotton frocks with white Peter Pan collars.

The majority of the games described here would have been played – or are played – in the earlier years, during primary school and during the first year or so of secondary education.

Blindman's Bluff

Also known as Blindman's Buff, this is a traditional game which entails blindfolding one child, who must then try to catch the other players. They will call to bait them, or to let them know where they are, or will tug at their clothes and hands. When the blindfolded child catches someone, they must guess their identity.

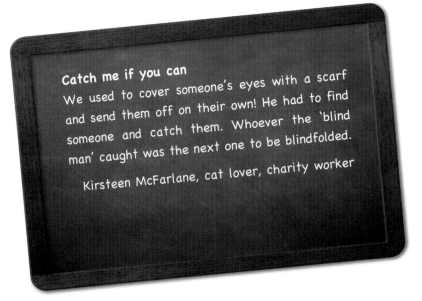

Catch me if you can
We used to cover someone's eyes with a scarf and send them off on their own! He had to find someone and catch them. Whoever the 'blind man' caught was the next one to be blindfolded.

Kirsteen McFarlane, cat lover, charity worker

British Bulldog

This popular game can get quite rough, and there are many versions. One of the most common is played with the children forming two lines some distance apart, while the Bulldog stands in the middle. At a given signal, the players rush across to the other side, while the Bulldog (sometimes two of them) try to catch someone before they reach sanctuary. Often, the player who is caught has to be held down on the ground for a count of 10, or sometimes lifted by the Bulldog so that both feet are off the floor, for a similar count, or maybe while the Bulldog shouts 'British Bulldog'.

Vicious dog
A favourite, though politically incorrect nowadays, was British Bulldogs!

Peter Andrews, avid collector, writer

British Bulldog was banned at our school because it was too fierce. We didn't have a Bulldog, we just formed lines opposite each other and then all ran at once, trying to catch each other. People got hurt.

Kirsteen McFarlane, cat lover, charity worker

We used to play British Bulldog 1,2,3, which unfortunately resulted one day in my losing a front tooth, after it was knocked out by the broom that my over-enthusiastic brother was wielding to stop us getting across!

Karen Conn, devoted mum from Worcestershire

Can I Cross Your Shining River?

A group of children choose one player to be Mr Crocodile, then they form a line in front of the chosen player and chant "Hey, Mr Crocodile, can I cross your shining river?" Mr Crocodile (choosing a colour) replies "Only if you are wearing red!" Any of the children wearing red can move one step. This is repeated many times, with Mr Crocodile choosing various colours, until a player finally reaches the agreed finishing point. Then that player becomes Mr Crocodile.

This is one of those games with numerous variations, one of the most popular being "Farmer, Farmer, may we cross your golden river?" The farmer calls out a colour and anyone wearing it can cross to the agreed finishing line, but those who don't have the colour must rush across trying to evade the Farmer. Any child they catch is out. The children, now on the line, must make their request again, and the Farmer chooses another colour, and so the sequence is repeated.

Of course, sometimes the children are all in school uniform, and so won't have many colours, in which case the Farmer might allow all those who own a pet dog, or who ate toast for breakfast, or who have a younger sister, to cross safely.

Chinese Whispers

Particularly effective when a lot of children play. They form a line or a circle, and one person whispers a sentence into their neighbour's ear. The sentence is whispered all around in turn, until it finally reaches the last person, who will then repeat it. Not only is it interesting to see how much the sentence is altered, it also demonstrates just how news and gossip become widespread and unreliable!

Colours

This game is almost the same as Letters (see p75). The chosen caller or It has to call out a colour, and if any of the children in the line have that colour on their clothing (or underclothing), they take a step forward. Those wearing multi-coloured cardigans always had the advantage in this game! The one who reaches the caller first touches them, then races back to the others. If the caller catches them, then they change places. If not, then the first caller will go to the front again and call more colours.

Crab Game

Children arch their backs and walk on their hands and feet sideways towards a chosen goal, maybe a wall or a litter basket. The winner is the first to reach it.

Dead Lions

Everyone lies down in the playground without moving. One child is It and they move around from child to child looking for twitches or any movement. Anyone who moves is out, and the winner is the last child left motionless. Apparently, this game was a great favourite with harassed teachers and playground ladies at several infants schools, as not only was it quiet and peaceful but, if they were very lucky, some of the children would doze off!

Drop the Handkerchief

(See also I Sent A Letter, chapter 2)

The children form a circle facing inwards, and one child is chosen as It. It walks, skips or runs around the outside of the circle carrying a handkerchief. It unobtrusively drops the hanky behind one of the children, then runs as fast as they can around the circle. The 'victim' grabs the hanky, jumps up and runs after It. It tries to get back to the victim's place, but if the victim manages to catch It, then It has to repeat the game. If It manages to reach the vacant place, then the victim becomes It.

Handkerchief games

Drop the Handkerchief was a circle game. We would join hands and form a circle, then drop our hands standing outside of the circle, with all our eyes on It and checking behind us as she passed to see if she'd dropped the handkerchief there. Usually she would begin running as soon as she dropped it - a big clue. You had to pick up the handkerchief before you could run after her. If tagged she had to repeat the process, if she made it back to the spot where she had dropped the handkerchief and slid into place before being tagged she was safe, and the chaser became the one dropping the handkerchief. Oh, and if the circle was smallish, we often went around more than once just to get someone off guard, and several of my classmates used to hum as they walker - more innocent?

Jo Birch, age 72, enjoys life to the full!

Duck, Duck, Goose

The children sit in a circle facing each other. One person is chosen as It and walks around the outside of the circle. It taps the players' heads as they pass, and says whether they are a Duck or a Goose. When they name someone as a Goose, the Goose gets up and chases them around the circle. The aim is to touch It before It reaches the Goose's spot and sits down. If the Goose can't do this, then Goose become It. If Goose touches It, then they stay as It for the next round.

An alternative version is played as above, but if Goose manages to touch It, It sits in the centre of the circle, leaving Goose as It. The former It stays in the middle until another person has been caught and touched, then they are replaced.

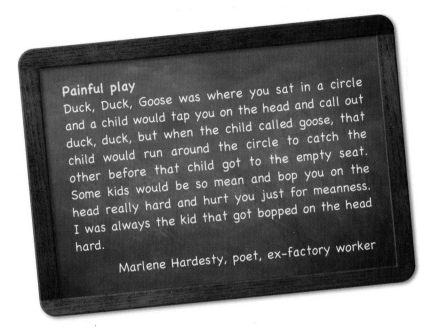

Painful play
Duck, Duck, Goose was where you sat in a circle and a child would tap you on the head and call out duck, duck, but when the child called goose, that child would run around the circle to catch the other before that child got to the empty seat. Some kids would be so mean and bop you on the head really hard and hurt you just for meanness. I was always the kid that got bopped on the head hard.

Marlene Hardesty, poet, ex-factory worker

Film Stars

Much loved in the 1950s-60s, Film Stars was a quick and easy game. One player was chosen to be It, normally through the usual dipping routines. The others would form a line, with It standing facing them some distance away. Then It would say the initials of a popular film actor or personality of the day, such as DD (Doris Day) or TS (Tommy Steele). If a player believed they knew the name, they would rush as fast as they could to It to whisper their guess. If they were right, they changed places and became It, if they were wrong, they had to run all the way back again. Of course, the mode of play did allow for a little cheating – after all, if It had decided on the initials DD for Doris Day, and the right answer was guessed early in the game, it wasn't unknown for It to protest that they were actually thinking of Diana Dors – or even Deanna Durbin!

Follow My Leader

A classic, easily begun, game which can be played with a minimum of two children – and a maximum of however many want to join in! Basically, one child is chosen as Leader, and the other children must do what they do as they lead them around the playground. They hop, jump, skip, walk backwards, touch a post, touch the ground, dance or wave their arms.

Grandmother's Footsteps
An old game, which begins with the ritual of choosing It. When they have been chosen It stands with their back to the rest of the children some distance away. The aim is to creep up on them without being spotted. It turns round every so often to try to spot a moving child – if they do, they call their name and order them back to the start. The winner of the game is the child who touches It without them seeing. Then they become It and the game begins again.

Handstands and Cartwheels
Especially loved by girls, handstands would be performed after chanting the ritual: Knife, fork, spoon, spear.

A crowd of boys invariably gathered to watch, as the girls' dresses or skirts would fall, revealing their knickers.

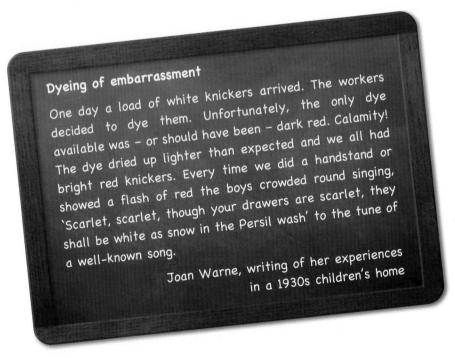

Dyeing of embarrassment

One day a load of white knickers arrived. The workers decided to dye them. Unfortunately, the only dye available was – or should have been – dark red. Calamity! The dye dried up lighter than expected and we all had bright red knickers. Every time we did a handstand or showed a flash of red the boys crowded round singing, 'Scarlet, scarlet, though your drawers are scarlet, they shall be white as snow in the Persil wash' to the tune of a well-known song.

Joan Warne, writing of her experiences in a 1930s children's home

Cartwheels were more difficult to perform properly, as the legs had to be held straight. Also, a cartwheeling child could be a bit of a liability in a crowded playground. Arab Springs were similar to a cartwheel, except that both feet were landed together.

Hide and Seek

This very simple game is sometimes played at school if the playground has hiding places – bins, posts, walls, doors or play equipment can all be pressed into service while, sometimes, one child will just crouch behind another. The Seeker covers their eyes and slowly counts to sixty before announcing, 'Ready or not, here I come' or 'Coming', or suchlike. In its basic form, the game is over when the first child is found, who then becomes the next Seeker. Sometimes, though, the Seeker has to find all the children, and frequently they will call out to taunt them, or cry 'cuckoo'.

If, after a while, not all the players can be found, or maybe the game is over because lessons are about to start, a traditional cry goes up of 'Allee Allee In', or 'Come out, come out, wherever you are', and when this is heard, it means a truce. It would be considered most unfair if the Seeker uttered the cry, then pounced as the children appeared from their hiding places.

Where Are You?
Hide and Seek was exciting. We gave the Seeker two minutes and everyone ran off and hid. It was very exciting when the Seeker found us.

Kirsteen McFarlane,
cat lover, charity worker

Hopscotch

There are various kinds of grids used, but the one most usually seen is drawn on a one square/two square/one square format with nine or ten squares in total. At the top it sometimes says 'home'. In London in the 1950s, when I was a child, the grids drawn were a rectangle divided into ten, two squares wide. At the top was written OXO!

Whichever grid pattern is drawn (traditionally, chalked onto the pavement), the game consists of children taking turns to throw a flat stone onto the grid, aiming to get it first on the square marked 1, the next on 2, etc, and hopping each time along the grid, hopping over the pebble to home and back again, picking up the pebble on the return journey. The one square/two square format allows the hopper to put both feet down on the double squares, while the rectangular grid means that the whole game is performed on one leg. Hoppers are out if they hop on the square containing the stone, or on a line. Some versions of the game allow players to chalk their initials in a chosen square, meaning that no other players must put their feet on it, but this can make the game difficult, especially when there are a large number of children.

A variation on hopscotch is played with a ball, which is bounced in the square the correct number of times. Occasionally the squares are drawn out as in circular

shape, or as a spiral, and the hopping is done on one foot only – if two feet are put down, the player is out.

Recently, police in Kent rushed to the scene when they were contacted with a report of graffiti being drawn on the road. They discovered that young children had marked out a hopscotch grid using chalk, so that they could play the traditional game. The children were quite frightened when the police arrived though, technically, no crime had been committed as chalk isn't permanent.

Some schools have ready-painted hopscotch grids in the playground.

Lost past

A friend said his daughter – an infants' teacher – told him that recently a day was held to coach teachers in explaining to young pupils how to play hopscotch and other games. Don't children learn from their siblings and peers now?

Doris Howe, retired playgroup supervisor, Suffolk

I really enjoyed marking a hopscotch grid with an old stone on our school playground floor. The joy of drawing on the playground floor inevitably made our hopscotch grid hopelessly elaborate.

Peter Andrews, avid collector, writer

I liked hopscotch because I used to tuck my circular skirt and red petticoat up into my frilly knickers!

Alison Sibley, talented artist, W. Sussex

Hopscotch was a game I loved to play alone; although group games are wonderfully interactive, the fact that it is always yours can be fun. Many hours were spent trying to better my last score. I remember how important it was to me to use a stone to throw on the ground that was aesthetically pleasing to me to look at and touch. I love and collect stones to this day. We lived in an area with a lot of natural chalk so I don't remember using chalk from a pack to draw my hopscotch grid, only the natural stuff, which had interesting shapes and left a residue on your fingers.

Trish Maunder,
freelance art educator, mum of two

Horsey

We used to play galloping horses by tying rope reins around each other and galloping around the playground, one player as the 'rider' holding the reins of a 'horse'.

Malcolm Brewer, retired customs officer, steam train fanatic, Essex

I Draw a Snake on the Elephant's Back

One child is chosen as the elephant and stands with his back to the others, while someone 'draws' a snake with their finger on his back. The first child then turns round and tries to guess who drew the snake.

I Spy

A classic, simple game which can be played at a moment's notice, and which tends to start spontaneously when someone suddenly says, 'I spy, with my little eye, something beginning with "C"' (or some other letter). The other players call out their ideas, often not taking turns – this isn't really an organised game. 'Coat!' 'Cloud!', 'Chaffinch!' 'Clock', until the word is guessed. Teachers approve of this game, because it teaches both spelling and vocabulary, and small children soon learn that, for instance, 'Ceiling' begins with a C and not an S!

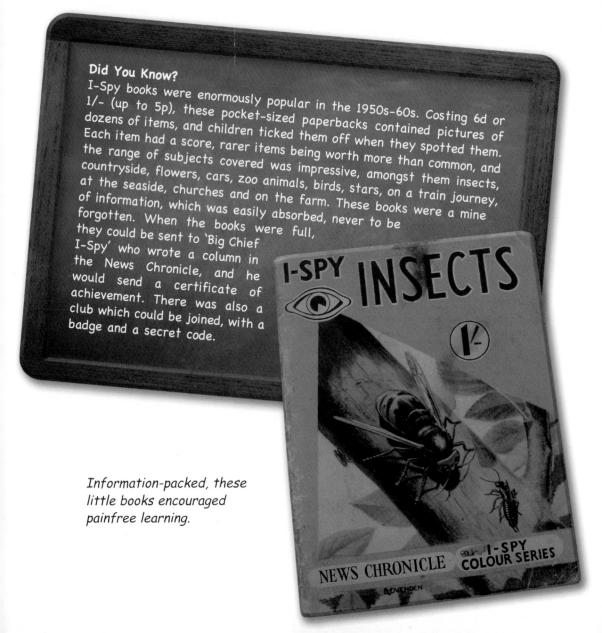

Did You Know?

I-Spy books were enormously popular in the 1950s–60s. Costing 6d or 1/- (up to 5p), these pocket-sized paperbacks contained pictures of dozens of items, and children ticked them off when they spotted them. Each item had a score, rarer items being worth more than common, and the range of subjects covered was impressive, amongst them insects, countryside, flowers, cars, zoo animals, birds, stars, on a train journey, at the seaside, churches and on the farm. These books were a mine of information, which was easily absorbed, never to be forgotten. When the books were full, they could be sent to 'Big Chief I-Spy' who wrote a column in the News Chronicle, and he would send a certificate of achievement. There was also a club which could be joined, with a badge and a secret code.

Information-packed, these little books encouraged painfree learning.

Keen readers of the I-Spy books joined the club and received a badge.

Keeper of the Stones

A chalk circle is drawn and one child (the keeper) stands in the middle. Everyone else forms a ring outside the circle and each places a stone inside. The aim is to retrieve a stone without getting tagged by the keeper.

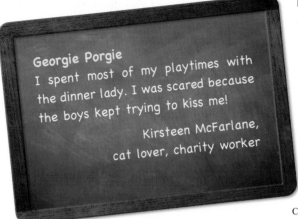

Georgie Porgie
I spent most of my playtimes with the dinner lady. I was scared because the boys kept trying to kiss me!

Kirsteen McFarlane,
cat lover, charity worker

Kiss Chase

A game often initiated by the girls, and disliked by the boys who 'have to kiss the girls', though by the age of 12 or so, both sexes enjoy it. Different regions have different rules, but usually a group of boys chase after the girls. When they catch one, she must struggle (albeit half-heartedly) to get away, while the boy takes her to the spot designated as 'home' and demands (or gives) a kiss. The girl is meant to then stay in that place till all the girls have been caught, but many, enjoying the thrill of the chase, will run off, to be caught again. Apparently, this is a very old game, a favourite, according to social historians Iona and Peter Opie of Eighteenth Century farm workers (*Children's Games* in *Street* and *Playground*, OUP 1969).

Kiss chase has been banned by a Lincolnshire school as it can be 'too rough'. The head teacher said that the children had been copying 'violent elements' of computer games and television shows, and has also banned tag (see chapter 6).

Leapfrog

The children form a line, bending over with their hands on their knees. One player tries to leap over every child. When they reach the end, they bend down, then it's the next person's turn to be the leapfrog.

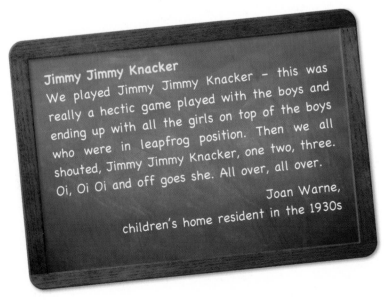

Jimmy Jimmy Knacker
We played Jimmy Jimmy Knacker – this was really a hectic game played with the boys and ending up with all the girls on top of the boys who were in leapfrog position. Then we all shouted, Jimmy Jimmy Knacker, one two, three. Oi, Oi Oi and off goes she. All over, all over.

Joan Warne,
children's home resident in the 1930s

Letters

A child is chosen to stand in front of a line of children, and they call out a letter of the alphabet. Any in the line who have that letter in their name take one step forward for the number of times it appears (middle names can also be taken into consideration), and the caller continues to call out letters until someone finally makes enough steps to reach the caller. Whoever gets there first becomes the next caller.

Mother, May I?

Once It is chosen, they stand some way away from the other children across the playground. The rest stand in a line facing them. The object of the game is for the children to reach It; the first that does, becomes It. There are many ways of playing this game, one way is for It to call out the name of one of the children and instruct them to take a certain amount of strange steps, such as giant, baby, crab, ballet or bunny hop. Another version has the children asking 'Mother, may I take three steps?' or similar, until they reached It or 'Mother'. Mother can allow or deny their request.

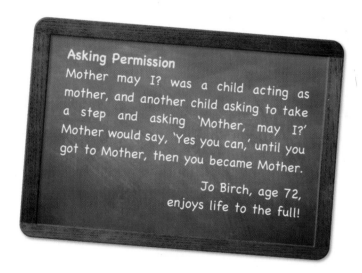

Asking Permission

Mother may I? was a child acting as mother, and another child asking to take a step and asking 'Mother, may I?' Mother would say, 'Yes you can,' until you got to Mother, then you became Mother.

Jo Birch, age 72, enjoys life to the full!

Murder

The children all sit in a ring, apart from one who is chosen as the detective. The detective goes out of earshot while the others choose a murderer. The detective then walks outside the circle, trying to find the murderer. Meanwhile, the murderer winks at a child who 'dies' spectacularly. Then they wink at another and so on. The aim is for the detective to catch the murderer before all the others are dead. If the detective catches the murderer, then the murderer becomes the detective.

Please, I've Come to Learn a Trade

This simple miming game kept children amused for some time. It probably dates from the 1920s/30s. The first child would mime an occupation, such as a window-cleaner, ice-cream salesman or cook, and the other child had to guess what it was. They took it in turns to be the one who wanted to learn the trade

Child 1: Please, I've come to learn a trade

Child 2: What trade?

Child 1: Any trade

Child 2: Get to work and do it then!

(Child 1 mimes the profession they want to enter).

Shipwrecks

In this game, you must keep off the ground – or 'sea' – by keeping to manhole covers, seats, lines on the playground, walls or holding onto drainpipes, while It keeps a lookout and aims to catch any child who puts a foot wrong when running from one 'island' to the next.

A variation is played by attempting to navigate the playground without stepping on any part of it.

Simon Says

This one is Follow My Leader with a difference. One player is chosen as Simon, and the other must do as Simon says – as long as he says 'Simon says' in his commands. If he just gives the command, and a child does what he says, then they are out. For instance, 'Simon says touch your nose' – all the children must comply.

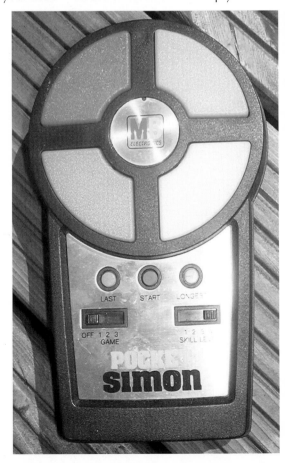

But if he just says, 'Touch your nose', then the children must stand still and not do anything. The winner is the person who remains at the end – this game can last all break time as the children try to catch each other out.

Sometimes this game is known as Mrs Grundy Says. Mrs Grundy was a character in *Speed the Plough*, a play written by Thomas Morton in 1798, and has become cited as a prudish or killjoy person. The name is still bestowed on a priggish or pompous woman – or man.

In the 1980s, an electronic game called Simon was very popular. Invented by Ralph H. Baer and Howard J. Morrison, it was distributed by Milton Bradley and has become something of a cult game. Basically, the idea was to follow a sequence of sounds and coloured flashing lights by touching various buttons on the game – a form of Simon Says.

KEEP STILL – Don't wobble.

Statues

Although really a party game, played with music, this was sometimes played in the school playgrounds. Children would run or dance, with one child (usually one who wasn't too self-conscious!) singing, then stopping suddenly. The others instantly froze, and anyone who wobbled, moved or twitched, was out. The winner was the last person left. Then they would become the singer. If you were very shy you were allowed to 'la la', hum, or even clap in a rhythm.

Television-influenced Games

Games are often fashion-led. In the 1950s, children played What's My Line?, based on a popular panel game of the time. Amongst the panel were Barbara Kelly (a glamorous actress with flashy earrings) and Gilbert Harding (a grumpy old actor). The show was presented by Eamonn Andrews, an Irishman with twinkly eyes. The aim was to guess, from mime, a person's occupation, and inevitably one child would take the Barbara Kelly role, with earrings fashioned from daisies or paper loops, while another would be the grouchy Gilbert Harding. The 'presenter' would attempt an Irish accent!

Other popular shows which lent themselves to play were Davy Crockett, Robin Hood and any of the westerns of the day, such as The Cisco Kid, Lone Ranger,

Wyatt Earp, Rawhide or Roy Rogers. By the 1960s, children were all Daleks from *Doctor Who* – 'Exterminate, Exterminate!' – the 1970s and 1980s led to imaginative play with space-centred TV/film programmes such as *Star Trek* or *Star Wars* (would you rather be Mr Spock or a Wookie?). The 1990s saw mini-playground episodes of soaps such as *EastEnders*, *Coronation Street* or *Neighbours*.

Nowadays, it's the reality shows that the children love – *Big Brother*, with one girl playing Davina McCall, – *Pop Idol*, *I'm a Celebrity Get Me Out of Here* (with lots of dares) – or the programmes searching for singers to fill popular musicals such as *Grease*. The aim of so many youngsters is 'to be famous, to be a star', that dance routines and songs are practised in playgrounds with no inhibitions, mock 'interviews' are conducted between interviewer and 'celeb' while 'catwalks' are marked out for aspiring models to sashay along. No one wants to be a nurse, air hostess, engine driver or teacher any more – but imagination is still wonderfully alive.

Playing the hero/ine

I used to play with my friends Martin and Janet in the late 1960s – Batman, Tarzan or Marine Boy. As I was an outgoing (bossy?) child and Janet was less so, I always used to choose who was Bat-Girl or Cat-Woman (usually myself) and who had a lesser starring role in our games. Worse though, whenever we played Tarzan I was always Jane to Martin's jungle hero, whilst Janet had to be Cheetah or Jai (in retrospect, I looked more like a cheetah than Janet did!)

Karen Conn, devoted mum from Worcestershire

Traffic Lights

In Red Light, Green Light, the caller had her back to you when she said "Green Light" and the children took large steps or ran, depending on the distance. The caller would suddenly say "Red Light" and whirl around trying to catch the someone moving, which is why big steps were often preferred. You could stop still standing with your legs stretched out in mid-step, just don't wobble! Those running, it was harder to stop mid-stride and they were often either the first to win, or the first to be caught and out. Those caught moving in any way were out of the game, so the field would get smaller and smaller and movement was easier to see. The first to reach the caller, or the last one standing, would be the next caller.

Jo Birch, age 72, enjoys life to the full!

We played Mother May I? and Red Light, Green Light and Duck Duck Goose. In Red Light Green Light you had someone call out "Green Light" and you would run as fast as you could before "Red Light" was called. When Red Light was called you had to stop in your tracks and when you got to the person calling the Red or Green Light you got to take that person's place. I tried to teach my kids the games, but they didn't want to play any of that old stuff!

Marlene Hardesty, poet, ex-factory worker

Three-legged Race

Two children tie their legs together with a scarf or a hanky, then try to run, their arms about each other. Great fun ensues as they try to co-ordinate their leg movements. This is another game often played in teams as a race.

Traffic Lights

Often known as Red Light, Green Light, It stands some way away from the other players, turns their back and calls 'Green Light'. The players run as fast as they can towards them, but if they turn and call, 'Red Light', they must instantly freeze. Anyone who doesn't stop is either out, or must go back to the start. The first player to reach It wins and becomes It. Variations include calling, 'Amber Light' when players must instantly crouch down.

There are versions which list other colours too, such as one which adds pink and purple. In this version, known as Rainbow Traffic Lights, red is stop, green is run, amber is sit down, purple is jump and pink is hop.

What's the Time, Mr Wolf?

A classic but potentially really scary game, which has the power to produce a spurt of fear, especially amongst five and six-year-olds. It begins with a bubble of anticipation, which builds and builds until

Fun or fear?

I had to laugh when my, almost, six year old daughter, Isabella, came home from school and proceeded to give me a breathless explanation of a new game they were playing that was "really really good Mummy – it's called What time is it Mr Wolf"! 40 years on and still being played!

Gail Caberlon, mum of two, loves reading

I certainly remember the terror of playing What's the time, Mr Wolf when the wolf turned around and screamed Dinnertime! The incredible high pitched noise of about twelve little girls all screaming at the top of their lungs!

Jean Needle, age 64, librarian/administrator

I think the game I disliked most was What time is it Mr Wolf, as I was always a bit scared when the wolf turned and tried to grab me.

Janet High, age 79, 'A Yorkshire Lass'

suddenly Mr Wolf turns and chases.

One child is chosen to be Mr Wolf, and they walk along, with the others following, and chanting 'What's the time Mr Wolf?' They turn to tell them the hour of the clock, and the children gradually grow bolder – until the wolf announces 'Dinnertime!' A mixture of terror and excitement is felt by each child as they run as fast as they can, pursued by the wolf. Whichever child the wolf catches will be the next Mr Wolf.

Another version has Mr Wolf facing the wall with the other children behind them so they can't be seen. The children advance a step for each hour Mr Wolf calls in answer to their eternal question, 'What's the time, Mr Wolf?'. When Mr Wolf has called enough hours for the children to be scarily close, the 'wolf' then turns and screams 'Dinnertime!' and catches the next Mr Wolf

What's the time Mr Wolf?
One o'clock.

What's the time Mr Wolf?
Four o'clock.

What's the time Mr Wolf?
Ten o'clock.

What's the time Mr Wolf?
Dinnertime!

Wheelbarrows

One child holds another's legs, pretending they are a wheelbarrow. The child who is the barrow uses their hands to propel themself while the pusher walks quickly or runs. This game is often turned into a race.

Wild Horses

Two or three children race about trying to gather a 'herd' of children willing to be horses. The child who has formed the largest herd of children is the winner.

Winter games

Winter days often caused ice to form over the asphalt playground, and someone, usually one of the older boys, would make a slide by the simple means of sliding in the same place several times until it was very smooth and very, very slippery. Sometimes there would be several slides across the playground, many schools used to forbid them because of the nasty accidents they often caused.

Other winter games included snowball fights, of course – they too were banned one year at my senior school after some people began throwing ice, rather than snow, which had small stones embedded into it. Children did occasionally try to make snowmen, but this was usually discouraged because the lunch break wasn't long enough to make a decent snowman, and so the playground would be scattered with piles of snow or solidifying large snowballs, which the long-suffering caretaker had to shovel away.

6. It or He

YOU CAN'T CATCH ME!

ALSO called Tag, It, Tig, Touch amongst dozens of other names. In its simplest form, He is chosen by dipping, then chases the other players. If He touches a player, then that player is 'had' and becomes He. Often, to goad He, various chants are called, such as:

> *Ha Ha Ha*
> *He He He*
> *You can't catch me*
> *For a toffee flea*
>
> *Ha Ha Ha*
> *He He He*
> *You can't catch me*
> *For a bumble bee*

Chain He

A variation of He in which the child who has been caught holds hands with He, and they run together. When the next child is caught, he holds hands with the player who is holding onto He, and so on, eventually forming a long chain.

Come out, come out...
In this game, whoever was It counted to a hundred while the others ran and hid. He then went in search of them. When one of the hiders was caught by him they joined him as a seeker and helped to find the others. As more kids were found, the search team got bigger. This went on until there was only one hider left and so became the winner. Sometimes, the others had to find him or her to convince them that they were actually the only one not yet found! They would ignore calls in case it was skulduggery by the seekers.

Barry Carter,
retired publican, Bethnal Green

Hidey He

It is chosen and, while they count (usually to a hundred, or recite a verse or 'mantra'), the other players run off to find hiding places. It then tries to find people and, when found, they also become It. Eventually, lots of Its are searching for the players, until they are all found. Sometimes, if one player finds a particularly good place to hide, the other searchers will get bored and wander off to play a new game, leaving the last person unsure whether they are still being sought!

Sticky Toffee

This is a game with lots of names. and very similar to Chain He. One person is chosen as He and when they touch someone, they

Melting Candles
[My daughter] Amy has a new playground game. It's called Melting Candles – there's lots of candles and one 'fire' who chases after the candles. When one is caught, she starts to 'burn' down to the ground and unless another candle 'puts her out' before she reaches the ground, she's out of the game. Apparently it's all the rage in the playground at the moment!

Kathy Martin,
arctophile extraordinaire, Berks

link hands and both run to find the next 'victim'. The victim links hands and so on, until a long chain has formed. Only the people on each end of the chain can touch, or tag, and only by using their free hands. If the chain breaks, it must quickly reform as, while broken, no one else can be caught.

Getting stuck.

Sticky Toffee 2

It is chosen in the usual way through dipping. They stand with their hands outstretched and fingers splayed. Each player takes hold of a finger. Then It begins to recite a 'shopping list'. For instance, they might say, 'I went to the shops and I bought a banana'. Then they might say, 'I went to the shops and I bought a banana and a loaf of bread'. Then, 'I went to the shops and I bought a banana and a loaf of bread and an apple.' And then, 'I went to the shops and I bought a banana and a loaf of bread and an apple and a bag of sticky toffee.' On the word 'toffee', everyone runs off – if a player lets go and runs off before the word toffee is said, then they become It. It tries to catch the other players. If a player is caught, they are stuck, and must stand with their arms out to the sides and their feet apart, as though glued to the playground. However, if another, free, player crawls through the legs of a stuck player, they are freed. The idea of the game is for It to get everyone stuck, and to guard them so they can't be freed.

Stone He

If a child is caught, they must 'turn to stone' and must stay like that until another player either crawls between their legs, touches their head, or, in some other previously decided way, breaks the 'spell', allowing them to be in the game again. The last player free becomes He.

Toucher/Colour Touch

There are many ways of playing this traditional game; the basic aim is for It to catch the players, but they can claim immunity by touching previously agreed items. These items vary, and are chosen according to what is available in the location. They might be things made from metal, from wood or from (in this modern age!) plastic. In Colour Touch, a colour is chosen, maybe red if the playground features red waste bins and seats, or green if the exterior doors are painted that colour, and children must run from one safe colour spot to another without being caught by It.

Truces

In many games, such as He, it is sometimes necessary for a player to stop – maybe they have cramp or a stitch, for example. There is a time-honoured code that a player who makes a certain sign or call, can be allowed a break without penalty. Sometimes a simple call of 'Truce' is used, but often it is a cry of 'Feignlights' (or Veinlights, or Feignights) accompanied by crossed fingers. Another cry frequently used is 'Kings' or 'Kingsys'.

Coming unstuck
[Sticky Toffee] was great fun to play but it was very difficult to free people when they were stuck, because the strategy was for It to guard them.

Jenna Brewer, born 1980, ballet and bunny enthusiast

Stuck on you
At Amy's school they play 'Stuck in the Mud' where the appointed 'stucker' (I've complained to her about the grammar but that's what they call it) immobilises anyone she catches until someone else touches them to 'unstuck' them. Other than that, they seem to prefer to play with their Tamagotchis at break time, or put on mock talent shows like the X-Factor.

Kathy Martin, arctophile extraordinaire, Berks

7. Childhood Nonsense

I BEG YOUR PARDON

FROM nonsense rhymes, loved by children the world over which have no meaning but can bring hours of innocent enjoyment, to cruel taunts, the language of childhood is universal.

Who, what, where?

> What's your name?
> Mary Jane (or Penny Lane, Puddin' Tame, Johnny Maclean)
>
> Where do you live?
> In a sieve (or Down the lane, Cabbage Lane)
>
> What's your address?
> Watercress
>
> What's your number?
> Cucumber
>
> What's your shop?
> Lollipop
>
> What's your age?
> Greengage

When someone says they don't care

> Don`t care was made to care
> Don`t care was hung
> Don`t care was put in a pot
> Till he was done.

When someone says they are hungry

> England was Hungary
> Had a bit of Turkey
> On a bit of China
> Dipped in Greece.

Used after burping

I beg your pardon
Mrs Arden,
But two of my pigs
Are in your garden.

When a girl's petticoat is showing

These cries seem to have died out by the late 1960s – by then, the petticoat was becoming an unfashionable item of clothing. The last version is one of those obscure sayings difficult to source, though one school of thought dates it from the beheading of Charles I in 1649. Oliver Cromwell forbade public mourning, but the King's friends had been allowed to dip their lace handkerchiefs in the King's blood (the rabble assembled at the execution followed suit without permission). It then became the fashion for ladies to display a lace petticoat hem beneath their skirts, as an insult to Cromwell. The ladies whispered, 'Charlie's dead' to each other, in his memory. The phrase gradually became accepted as a crude way of informing a woman that her petticoat was showing

It's snowing down south
Mrs White is out
Charlie's dead!

CHILDHOOD TAUNTS

A less pleasant aspect of the playground is bullying, often based on appearances or perceived differences. Today, some of these rhymes would not be tolerated, especially those which mock disabilities. They play on the playground pack, isolating individuals and the incessant nee-naw tone of the put-downs, combined with the child being surrounded or pushed against a wall by a large pack of children could be menacing

Aimed at a child who stares

Taunted with a repetitive tune which, if sang by a group of children, could be intimidating

> Stare cat, stare cat
> Don't know what you're looking at.
>
> Hair cut, hair cut
> Don't know what you're looking at.
>
> Made you look
> Made you stare
> Made the barber
> Cut your hair.
> He cut it long
> He cut it short
> He cut it with a knife and fork.

For a child with long hair

Plays on children's fear of the barber or painful haircuts at home with pudding bowls and blunt knives

> Cut his hair
> With a leg of a chair
> Cut it long
> Cut it short
> Cut it with a knife and fork.

For a child with a dirty face

> Dan Dan
> Dirty old man
> Washed his face
> In the frying pan.

To a lisping child

A cruel childhood taunt

> Mummy thais I listhp
> Daddy thais I don't
> Do you think I listhp?

Hear me call my puth
Puth! Puth!
Do you think I listhp?

To a sneak

Tell Tale Tit
Your tongue shall be split
And all the little puppy dogs
Will come and have a bit.

To a coward

Cowardy Cowardy Custard
Come and eat some mustard!

Aimed at a redhead

The curse of the carrot, redheads are still relatively rare in most communities so the child would become an easy target and be called names ranging from 'carrot' to 'ginge'

Ginger you're barmy!
You joined the army
You'll never get a job with a rusty knob
Ginger you're barmy!

To a liar

Liar, liar,
Pants on fire.

To a scruffy child

Giddy Giddy Gout
Your shirt's hanging out
Five yards in and five yards out!

To a crying child

Sometimes, Baby Bunting in the last line is replaced by the crying child's name

Cry Baby Bunting!
Daddy's gone a-hunting
He's gone to buy a rabbit skin
To put the Baby Bunting in.

To children in a line

First the worst
Second the best
Third the one with the hairy chest.

General taunts

Ha Ha Ha
He He He
You've got a face
Like a chimpanzee.

Sally Thompson is no good!
Chop her up for firewood!
Dunce, Dunce, Double D
Doesn't know his ABC.

Mind your own business

The following is attributed to the Eighteenth Century poet, Oliver Goldsmith

Ask me no questions
And I'll tell you no lies.

Curiosity killed the cat
Satisfaction brought it back.

I know a secret
I mustn't tell
I was born
In a walnut shell.

Iko Iko

Originally called Jock-a-mo, this popular challenging song was written in 1959 for the Mardi Gras in New Orleans and has many versions, including 'set your flags on fire'. It has been covered by many musicians, including the Dixie Cups and Cyndi Lauper and has featured in several films, including Rain Man and Mission Impossible. Iko Iko is Cajun patois and means something like 'listen!'. Jock-a-mo, its original title is a Native American victory chant, perfect for playground challenges – my one's better than your one!

My grandpa and your grandpa
Sitting by the fire
My grandpa to your grandpa
I'm going to set your pants on fire.
(Sometimes the chorus was chanted:
Iko, Iko, Iko Iko one day
Iko iko up there
Iko Iko one day.)

8. Ball Games

IT'S MY BALL AND I'M GOING HOME

ONE OF the most popular playground games is, of course, football, but that really falls into a sporting category so won't be included here. Other sporting games include rounders or French cricket, both of which tend to be more organised pastimes which take a long while to play, rather than the spontaneous games which evolve and can be completed within the short playtime or lunch break period.

Practically from birth, children are given a ball to play with – at first, it will probably be made from colourful soft cloth, or plastic with a chime inside. It may be one of a set threaded onto an elastic cord stretched across a pram, or perhaps a rubbery one with a bell inside. Soon, though, it will be a ball the child can learn to throw, and then to catch and, by the time they reach school age, various ball games will have been at least attempted, if not mastered.

The simplest of toys.

Ball wall

Playground walls have long been the mainstay of children's games. Perfect for throwing balls against, of course, or using for tennis practice by hitting balls with a tennis racquet against them (at the senior school I attended, many a lunch break was spent in this way), walls were also 'home' or feignlights, and provided places to flick cigarette cards, roll marbles at, chalk on, climb up, jump off, lean against or to use as a meeting point. But best of all, they were for ball games, because they enabled a single player to get the ball to rebound, and, unlike a ball-returning partner, would never tire!

*Ball games teach
co-ordination.*

*Catch it on
the rebound.*

Bad Eggs

This game needs a small ball, such as a tennis ball, and a person who is It. It chooses a subject, such as colours, cars, film stars or countries, and the others decide what they will be from that chosen category (e.g. yellow if colour is the chosen subject), without letting It overhear. One person then tells It the chosen names, without letting them know who has chosen what, and It throws the ball into the air, calling out a word (such as yellow, if that is the chosen category). The person whose colour has been chosen, runs to catch the ball while everyone else runs away. When they have caught the ball, they call 'Bad Eggs'. Everyone – including the person with the ball – stands still, and all, except the catcher, stand with their legs apart. The catcher is allowed to take three big steps towards any child they want and then roll the ball, aiming to get it through that child's legs. If they manage to do so, then the child, whose legs the ball went through, is It. Otherwise, the catcher becomes It. This game is much easier to play than to describe!

What a bad egg!

Egga needed a tennis ball in order to play. As usual the one to be It was picked by 'dipping'. The person who was It would give the rest of the group a subject to choose a name from. The group then huddled together and chose names from the given subject. If the choice was colours, then one would pick blue, another red, and so on. One person would then recite all the chosen colours to the one who was It, who then threw the ball high into the air against the wall shouting out loud one of the colours given to them. Whoever had chosen that colour had to retrieve the ball while the others ran away. As soon as they caught it they shouted, "Egga", and everyone had to stand still. The person with the ball was then allowed three giant steps towards any one of the others, and threw the ball to hit them, making them It and the whole cycle started again.

Barry Carter,

retired publican, Bethnal Green

Ball Tag

This is a variation of Tag, He or It. After It has been chosen, normally through the usual counting out/dipping rhymes process, the players run. It holds a ball, and throws it as they run. If they hit someone, then that person becomes It instead.

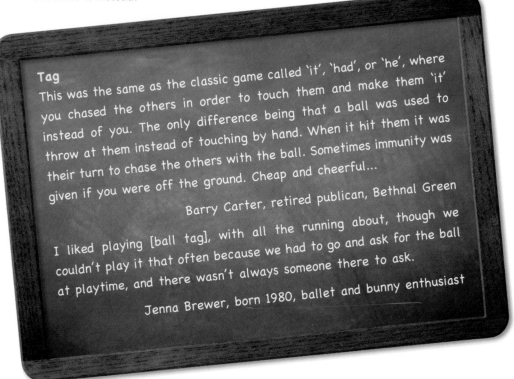

Tag

This was the same as the classic game called 'it', 'had', or 'he', where you chased the others in order to touch them and make them 'it' instead of you. The only difference being that a ball was used to throw at them instead of touching by hand. When it hit them it was their turn to chase the others with the ball. Sometimes immunity was given if you were off the ground. Cheap and cheerful...

Barry Carter, retired publican, Bethnal Green

I liked playing [ball tag], with all the running about, though we couldn't play it that often because we had to go and ask for the ball at playtime, and there wasn't always someone there to ask.

Jenna Brewer, born 1980, ballet and bunny enthusiast

Call Ball

The children sit in a circle, and they pass around a ball as they chant the following rhyme. The child holding the ball when the letter 'U' is called, is out of the game, and must sit with their hands behind their back. The game continues until there is only one person left, and, as more and more children are eliminated, it gets harder to pass the ball, often necessitating throwing if the children are too far from each other to just pass it. This game can also be played standing

The shiny ball goes round and round
To pass it quickly, you are bound
But if it's you who holds it last,
Now the game for you has passed
Out goes Y-O-U!

Circle Ball

The children form a circle and a small ball, such as a tennis ball is thrown by one child to the child opposite, who throws it to the child standing to the right of the first thrower. This child throws the ball to the child opposite, who throws it to the right of the last child and so on, moving around the circle as quickly as possible. If a child is out, then he places his hands behind his back but keeps his place. As the game progresses, everyone must keep track of who is in and who is out, so that the ball doesn't get dropped.

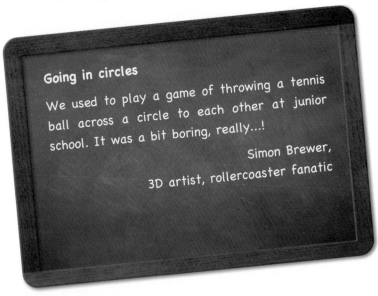

Going in circles

We used to play a game of throwing a tennis ball across a circle to each other at junior school. It was a bit boring, really...!

Simon Brewer,

3D artist, rollercoaster fanatic

Keep the ball moving.

Counting rhymes

The children take turns at bouncing the ball, while everyone chants the rhyme. On the word 'O'Lary', the player lifts one leg up and over the ball as it bounces, before continuing to bounce the ball. If the player loses the rhythm and drops the ball, the next person takes a turn

One, two, three O'Lary
Four, five, six O'Lary
Seven, eight, nine O'Lary
Ten O'Lary boys.

A more difficult version is performed using a bouncing ball to the chant below, with the leg being lifted over the ball on the word 'little'

One little, two little, three little Indians
Four little, five little, six little Indians
Seven little, eight little, nine little Indians
Ten little Indian boys.

This next verse was chanted by children as they played 'two-ball' (throwing two tennis balls against a wall, see p100)

One, two, three and plainsie
Four, five, six and oversie
Seven, eight, nine and upsie
Ten and dropsie, start again.

Dodge Ball or Kingy

This can be quite a fast-moving game and probably appeals to boys more than girls. The aim of the game is to hit another child with a ball. One child is chosen as Kingy (or It) and the other players scatter. Kingy throws the ball as hard as possible in the direction of one of the children, who tries to dodge the ball or punch it away. If, however, the ball hits them, they join Kingy in throwing the ball at other players. Eventually, the majority of the players have joined Kingy, and they circle the remaining few. The ball will be mercilessly thrown at them by the players in league with Kingy, until there is only one player left. They will be the next Kingy. There are dozens of variations of this game.

Donkey

A few children form a ring or square and throw a tennis-sized ball across from one to the other. If a child drops the ball instead of catching it, they lose a life – i.e. a 'D'. Next time it happens, they lose another life, an 'O', and so on until they have spelt out the word 'Donkey' – then they're out. This

Bruised pride

Oh, I hated 'Dodge Ball' – who wants to be hit by a ball?!! And some of the class could throw hard. Of course, that was in the lower classes before I went to the Catholic girls' school, where nothing like that was allowed!

Jo Birch, age 72,
enjoys life to the full!

game relies on children's honesty to keep their own scores – surprisingly, most children seem scrupulously fair about this.

Juggling

Juggling in the air with two, three or four balls was popular – not many of us managed the latter!

Janet High, age 79
'A Yorkshire Lass'

I used to chant this one while attempting to throw two balls against a wall, like simple juggling!

Nebuchadnezzar the King of the Jews
Bought his wife a pair of shoes.
When the shoes began to wear
Nebuchadnezzar began to swear.
When the swear began to stop
Nebuchadnezzar bought a shop.
When the shop began to sell
Nebuchadnezzar bought a bell.
When the bell began to ring
Nebuchadnezzar began to sing.
Doh Re Me Fa So La Te Doh.

I did it to skipping too, with 'bumps' on the doh re me etc part!

Joan Kinnock,
doll enthusiast, Gloucestershire

Piggy in the Middle

A quick and easy game for three children, two tossing the ball to each other, over the head of a third child who has to try to catch it. When the piggy catches the ball, it's the turn of the child who should have caught it to become piggy and stand in the middle. Occasionally, this game is played with more than two players, whilst the hapless piggy tries to catch the ball.

Whose ball is it, anyway?

Some of the games were known by different names in other parts of the town or country but all had basically the same rules. One of these rules concerned whose game it was. Obviously when playing a ball game the owner of the ball had the final word. "Can I play?" the latecomer would ask. "Better ask Billy, it's his ball", would be the reply. This rule had to be adhered to – otherwise Billy simply took his ball home and ended it.

Barry Carter, retired publican, Bethnal Green

Queenie, Queenie

Popular amongst primary school children in the 1950s and 1960s, there were various ways of playing this game, though the most frequently found was to choose a girl to be Queenie by dipping. Of course, if the ball belonged to her it was only fair that she had the first go at being Queenie.

Turning her back on a row of girls, Queenie would toss the ball in the air over her shoulder. The girls would run to catch it, and the winner would hide it behind her back. Then they would chant:

Queenie, Queenie, who's got the ball?
Is she big or is she small?

And Queenie would turn round and try to guess who had the ball. If she were right, then the girl who had the ball would become Queenie. If she were wrong, she remained Queenie.

Queenie, Queenie, who's got the ball?
Is she fat or is she small?
Is she thin or is she tall?
Queenie, Queenie, who's got the ball?

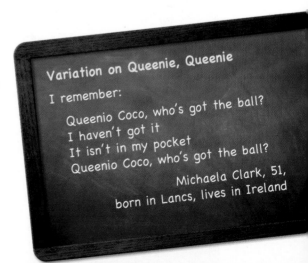

Variation on Queenie, Queenie

I remember:

Queenio Coco, who's got the ball?
I haven't got it
It isn't in my pocket
Queenio Coco, who's got the ball?

Michaela Clark, 51,
born in Lancs, lives in Ireland

Spuddy

There are several versions of this game. In one, children choose It by the usual counting out/rhyming ritual, then form a circle, standing shoulder to shoulder with It in the middle. If It knows the names of all the players, the game begins immediately, otherwise It counts around the circle, giving each child a number. Then they throw the ball high into the air and call out a player's name or number. That player must catch the ball, while the other children run. If they catch it, they call out 'Spuddy' (or, in a different version, their name or number), and are now It. All the others freeze, while the new It throws the ball at another player, trying to 'tag' them. If they are successful, that player gets an 'S' and becomes It. However, if the player catches the ball, then they get an 'S'. Target players must keep both feet on the ground, though are allowed to duck or catch. The game continues until a player builds up the word Spuddy (after being tagged six times). Then they are out. The game goes on until only one player is left – which can take quite a while if there are a lot of players.

Two Ball

A particularly popular playground game of the 1950s and 1960s – and earlier – was 'Two Ball' – basically, a simple juggling act performed by one child to assorted chants. Similar chants were used for patting bouncing balls or throwing them against a wall, often adapted from skipping chants. More ambitious children would try to keep a ball bouncing while stepping over it, moving it behind their back, closing their eyes or patting it in a circle all around their body.

Wounded Soldier

A small group of children form a ring, and the ball is thrown across the ring to the child opposite, who throws it to the child to right of the first person to throw, so that the ball reaches each child in turn. The aim is to catch the ball. If they drop it, they must place an arm behind their backs. If they drop it again when their turn next arrives, they must stand on one leg, then next time, kneel on one knee. Then on both knees. Then they are out. The winner is the last child still able to throw the ball. Sometimes, children add extra 'wounds' such as closing one eye, closing both eyes, or even both hands behind the back and catching the ball under the chin!

Who will catch it?

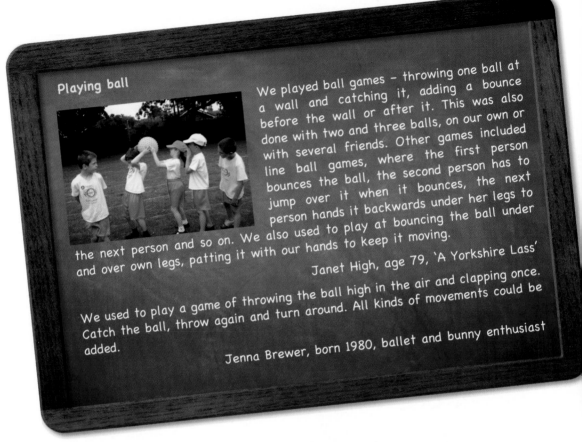

Playing ball

We played ball games – throwing one ball at a wall and catching it, adding a bounce before the wall or after it. This was also done with two and three balls, on our own or with several friends. Other games included line ball games, where the first person bounces the ball, the second person has to jump over it when it bounces, the next person hands it backwards under her legs to the next person and so on. We also used to play at bouncing the ball under and over own legs, patting it with our hands to keep it moving.

Janet High, age 79, 'A Yorkshire Lass'

We used to play a game of throwing the ball high in the air and clapping once. Catch the ball, throw again and turn around. All kinds of movements could be added.

Jenna Brewer, born 1980, ballet and bunny enthusiast

Throws and rhythm

There are many rhymes used to accompany ball games; often two balls are bounced against a wall, with various actions being performed on the rhyming words. Rhymes, of course, are essential to help the rhythm of the bouncing ball become established. Throws include:

Basic and tactile.

Overs – *Overhand throw*
Unders – *Underhand throw*
Uppys – *Throw the ball into the air*
Dropsys – *Throw the ball against the wall, let it drop and catch it when it bounces.*

Sometimes, these are played as a solo game but, more often, children take turns when the first player drops the balls. Often, if the player completes the whole sequence to the rhyme, they will begin again using just one hand. Typical rhymes include Tom Thumb

Each peach pear plum, where is Tom Thumb?
Tom Thumb is in the cellar, where is Cinderella?
Cinderella's in the wood, where is Robin Hood?
Robin Hood's upstairs, where are the three bears?

This rhyme is constantly added to, there are lots of variations. Often, the player will make up more verses as she plays.

Free play

Sometimes, a group of children would grab a bat, often a cricket bat, for a quick knock-around game during lunch break, not following a formal game which would take too long. Wooden bats and children can be quite a lethal combination!

Hand-eye co-ordination
I like playing with the ball because I know I can't catch it when I throw it against the wall, but it's quite funny when I do that!

Lucy White, age 6, loves dancing and gymnastics, Dorset

I like ball skills as I can catch with one hand. I like throwing it against the wall and catching it and jumping over it.

Holly White, age 8, plays piano and violin, enjoys dancing, Dorset

That's not cricket!
A playtime injury that I sustained was less of an accident – a dubious-charactered little boy whacked me over the head with a cricket bat! My mother only discovered what had happened when she lifted up my fringe to wash my face at bedtime and found that my forehead was coloured in all shades of purple, green, black and blue!

Karen Conn,
devoted mum from Worcestershire

If you drop it you're a donkey.

9. Clapping Games

PAT-A-CAKE

ONE OF the first games a baby learns is how to clap. Clapping games are deservedly popular with school children – they are fun, impromptu and many are accompanied by tongue-twisting rhymes. As children become more skilled, they can build up a tremendous speed, using complicated hand patterns and movements. Clapping teaches hand and eye co-ordination, as well as rhythm, and encourages children to concentrate – one mistake and the game will need to be restarted.

(See also p51 – counting-out rhymes)

Clapping

This is a word association game which goes on for as long as the players can come up with words. An ability to think quickly is needed. A clapping rhythm is set up amongst a group of children, often three claps and then a word is said, then three more claps before the next player says a word and so on. For instance, the first player might say bread, the next butter, the third cup (i.e. buttercup), the fourth saucer, the fifth flying, the sixth, bird – and the game continues, with the three claps between each word, giving the next player a brief time to come up with a word. If a word which has been already used is repeated, then that player is out. If a player can't think of a word, then they are out. When no-one can think of any more associated words, the game ends.

Rhythms and motions

There were two different types of clapping movement, some clapping was vertical and some horizontal. The games and rhythm could get quite complicated, and often sped up at the end.

Jenna Brewer,
born 1980, ballet and bunny enthusiast

It's important to match each other's rhythm.

Have You Ever, Ever, Ever?

Have you ever, ever, ever in your short-legged life
Seen a short-legged sailor with a short-legged wife?
No I've never, never, never in my short-legged life
Seen a short-legged sailor with a short-legged wife.

Have you ever, ever, ever in your long-legged life
Seen a long-legged sailor with a long-legged wife?
No I've never, never, never, in my long-legged life
Seen a long-legged sailor with a long-legged wife.

Have you ever, ever, ever, in your knock-kneed life
Seen a knock-kneed sailor with a knock-kneed wife?
No I've never, never, never in my knock-kneed life
Seen a knock-kneed sailor with a knock-kneed wife.

Have you ever, ever, ever, in your crooked-leg life
Seen a crooked-leg sailor with a crooked-leg wife?
No I've never, never, never in my crooked-leg life
Seen a crooked-leg sailor with a crooked-leg wife.

Have you ever, ever, ever in your pigeon-toed life
Seen a pigeon-toed sailor with a pigeon-toed wife?
No I've never, never, never in my pigeon-toed life
Seen a pigeon-toed sailor with a pigeon-toed wife.

Have you ever, ever, ever in your bow-legged life
Seen a bow-legged sailor with a bow-legged wife?
No I've never, never, never in my bow-legged life
Seen a bow-legged sailor with a bow-legged wife.

Have you ever, ever, ever in your short-legged life
Seen a short-legged sailor with a long-legged wife?

No I've never, never, never in my short-legged life
Seen a short-legged sailor with a long-legged wife.

Have you ever, ever, ever in your long-legged life
Seen a long-legged sailor with a short-legged wife?
No I've never, never, never, in my long-legged life
Seen a long-legged sailor with a short-legged wife.

Have you ever, ever, ever in your crooked-leg life
Seen a crooked-legged sailor with a knock-kneed wife?
No I've never, never, never in my crooked-leg life
Seen a crooked-legged sailor with a knock-kneed wife.

Have you ever, ever, ever, in your knock-kneed life
Seen a knock-kneed sailor with a crooked-leg wife?
No I've never, never, never in my knock-kneed life
Seen a knock-kneed sailor with a crooked-leg wife.

Have you ever, ever, ever in your pigeon-toed life
Seen a pigeon-toed sailor with a bow-legged wife?
No I've never, never, never in my pigeon-toed life
Seen a pigeon-toed sailor with a bow-legged wife.

Have you ever, ever, ever in your bow-legged life
Seen a bow-legged sailor with a pigeon-toed wife?
No I've never, never, never in my bow-legged life
Seen a bow-legged sailor with a pigeon-toed wife.

I went to…

Chinese restaurants were once seen as very exotic as they were a novel idea unlike today's multicultural offerings on every high street. There are several versions of this clapping game, most of which play on silly-sounding words

I went to a Chinese restaurant
To buy a loaf of bread, bread, bread.
He wrapped it up in a five pound note,
And this is what he said, said, said -
My name is Elvis Presley, girls are sexy
Sitting in the back room drinking Pepsi
I diddle I di – sexy!

I went to… 2

I went to a Chinese restaurant
To buy a loaf of bread, bread, bread.
He wrapped it up in a five pound note,
And this is what he said, said, said –
My name is Ely Ely, Chickali Chickali
Pom pom, poodle, wally wally whiskers
Chinese chopsticks, Indian tomatoes – how pow!

My Mother Said
Played by two children facing each other, alternatively clapping and slapping their hands

> *My mother said*
> *I never should*
> *Play with the gypsies*
> *In the wood.*
> *If I did*
> *She would say*
> *Naughty girl*
> *To disobey.*

Oom Pah
Many children's games are based on silly words, ideal for clapping rhythms

> *Oom pah vee, diddy vee, diddy ooshka*
> *Oom pah vee, follow me*
> *Yakadeena, so fah me*
> *Yakadeena, poof poof.*

Pat-a-cake
An infant's game, or nursery rhyme, this is a very old rhyme which dates back to the late 1600s and was originally sung to amuse babies. It is played with two children alternatively clapping and then placing their upraised left palm onto the left palm of her partner (standing opposite), then the right and so on. They chant a rhyme at the same time, trying to maintain the rhythm of both hands and words

> *Pat-a-cake, Pat-a cake*
> *Baker's man*
> *Bake me a cake as fast as you can.*
> *Prick it and pat it*
> *And mark it with B*
> *And put in the oven for baby and me.*

Hands up!

Pease Pudding

The cry of 'Pease pudding hot' once used to echo around the streets of London. It's a trader's call dating from the 1700s. Several chants were used to play the clapping game described in Pat-a-cake, including 'Pease pudding'

Pease pudding hot
Pease pudding cold,
Pease pudding in the pot
Nine days old.
Some like it hot
Some like it cold,
And some like it in the pot
Nine days old.

See See My Playmate

See see my playmate
I cannot play with you
My sister's got the flu
Chicken pox and measles too
All down the drain pipe
Into the kitchen sink.
I'll be your playmate
For ever more, more
Shut the door door
Don't come back till half past four.

See See My Playmate 2

See see my playmate
I cannot play with you
Because I've got the flu
Chicken pox and measles too
All down the drain pipe
Into the captain's ship.
I'll be your playmate
For ever more more
Shut the door
Don't come back till half past four.
Half past four is much too late
Don't come back till half past eight.

Susie

Saucy Susie made for a great clapping game as the children marked out her development – until the very end

When Susie was a baby,
A baby Susie was
She went cry, cry, cry, cry.
When Susie was a toddler,
A toddler Susie was
She went scribble, scribble, scribble, scribble.

When Susie was a child,
A child Susie was
She went why? why? why? why?

When Susie was a teenager,
A teenager Susie was
She went ooh, ahh, I lost my bra,
I left my knickers in my boyfriend's car.

When Susie was a mother,
A mother Susie was
She went bake, bake, bake, bake.

When Susie was a granny,
A granny Susie was
She went knit, knit, knit, knit.

When Susie was a skeleton,
A skeleton Susie was
She went (silence, stop clapping).

Under the Palm Bush

Under the palm bush down by the sea
Boom boom boom
Two lovers sitting in harmony
And when they marry, they'll raise a family.
One boy for you, my darling, one girl for me
Boom boom boom
Five foot two, eyes of blue
Hoochy coochy I love you!

10. Skipping and Chants

BUMPS AND GRINDS

CHILDREN have skipped for centuries: skipping and skipping games are part of most cultures. Over the years, hundreds of skipping games, chants and rhymes have evolved, passed down from mother to daughter. Whilst boys skip as well, they seem to prefer skipping games rather than skipping to rhymes. In days gone by, though, skipping would have been a man or boy's sport – girls wouldn't have pursued such a boisterous activity.

There used to be a 'skipping season' at school; the ropes would appear, in the spring, after the Easter holidays. Some girls would bring in their standard length ropes with painted wooden handles, but there was always someone who would

Simply the best – a traditional wooden-handled skipping rope.

1970s infants practise skipping.

acquire a long length of clothes' line so that several girls could skip at once. Two 'turners' would be chosen, usually by a dipping rhyme and the person who owned the rope was the first to skip, before the other girls joined in.

The girls were always scrupulously fair about taking turns, forming lines so they could quickly 'run in', skipping to whatever chant had been chosen by the turners. Chants varied region by region, though many were universally known. There were also skipping games such as Over the Moon and Under the Stars which necessitated the skippers taking it in turn to run under the rope or to jump over the rope, as it turned, and Colours, in which the skipper called the name of a colour as they ran into the rope.

Rhymes for one skipper using a short rope

These rhymes don't need actions, so can be performed by one child skipping alone. Some are purely rhymes to help with rhythm, whilst others involve counting or speeding up of the rope. Most children learn by using a standard rope, later graduating to skipping in a long rope, turned by others.

Bumps
Esau
Esau (2)
Esau (3)
Flies
Flu
I Had a Sausage
Jelly
Mabel
Mickey Mouse
Moses
Pumpkin
Sausages

Remember the rhyme – and don't forget to jump!

112

Jumping high.

Am I out?

One skipper at a time using a long rope with two turners
These rhymes need various actions, or require the skipper to continue until they are 'out' by tripping on the rope, or they just get tired

> *Bluebell, Cockleshell*
> *Charlie Chaplin*
> *Down by the Meadow*
> *Down by the River*
> *Down in the Valley*
> *Dutch Girl*
> *Fairy*
> *Girl Guide*
> *Rubber Dolly*
> *Teddy Bear*

Where skippers run in and out using a long rope with two turners

These rhymes are probably the most hectic of all, and involve plenty of (often fast) action. Skippers usually run in and out as their name, their birthday or the name of the character they are portraying is called. Sometimes, as one runs in, the other runs out, but often, such as in All in Together Girls, everyone apart from the turners ends up skipping in one glorious, synchronised free-for-all – as long as the rope is long enough, there is no limit to the number of skippers jumping the rope

All in Together Girls
Apples
Appreciate
Bubble Car
Coffee
I Had a Little Puppy
Miss Polly
Peter and Paul
There's Somebody under the Bed
Vote Vote Vote

Dodge the rope – rather lethal!

Group skipping

Many of the skipping chants can be used for group skipping or for solo skipping, but some can only be performed by groups as they require actions such as saluting, waving or touching the ground. None of these actions can be performed if a skipper is holding the handle of a rope in each hand! Other chants require people to run in and out of the rope, sometimes singly, changing places with the skipper, and sometimes ending up with all the children skipping together – which requires a very long rope.

Taking turns

Skipping was a game we girls enjoyed, and we had many skipping rhymes. Communal skipping was especially good as two girls were turners and all the others skipped in and out of the turning rope keeping the pot boiling. Bumps was another form of skipping to which we chanted a variety of rhymes. This was very fast skipping, performed mainly solo.

Joan Warne,
children's home resident in the 1930s

SKIPPING RHYMES

All in Together Girls

A favourite rhyme, this one is irresistible with its insistent beat. Once the turners begin their chant, girls come rushing, keen to run in as their birthday month is called

> *All in together, girls,*
> *Never mind the weather, girls.*
> *When it is your birthday,*
> *Please run in!*

January, February, March, April, May, June, July, August, September, October, November, December.

> *All in together, girls,*
> *Never mind the weather, girls.*
> *When it is your birthday,*
> *Please run out!*

January, February, March, April, May, June, July, August, September, October, November, December.

Jumping the rope.

All Together, Girls

One of my favourite playground memories is that of skipping in the warm summer playtimes which seemed to go on forever. We had a very long rope, an old discarded clothes line begged from someone's mum and took it in turns to wield the long rope around and around, a feat in itself! Chanting the song together, we sang through the months of the year until our birth month was called, then it was time to try and jump in without stopping the rope. My birthday was September so the space was quite limited by the time I joined the long line of children skipping in harmony. As we reached December, the chant changed and it was 'when I call your birthday please jump out'. Gradually, the rope emptied and that's when I got my best skips. Of course, everyone wanted to be friends with the girl who owned the skipping rope as quite often it was their decision who could play. I don't remember not being allowed to join in. Only happy memories.

Lesley Glover, ex-primary school teacher, enjoys knitting

Apples

In similar mode to All in Together
Girls, this begins with one skipper, with the others running in
on their birthday, then out again during the following verse when their birthday is
called

> Apples, peaches, pears and plums
> Tell me when your birthday comes.
> Apples, berries, nuts and sloes
> Tell me when your birthday goes.

Appreciate

This one begins with one person skipping, who runs out when the next girl is called, and so on. The rhyme is just repeated until a change of chant is decided upon

> Two, Four, Six, Eight
> Who do we Ap-pre-ci-ate?
> S, a, l, l, y
> Sally!

Bluebell, Cockleshell

One of those pretty rhymes, which dates back to the turn of the century or earlier – later skipping rhymes tend to be less fanciful. The rope was swung two and fro and then over in time with the words. The skipper had to jump the rope

> Bluebell, cockleshell
> Evie-ivy-over.

Charlie Chaplin

Charlie Chaplin initially started out as a star of the silent movies, but made a successful transition to the 'Talkies'. His heyday was the 1930s, and this chant probably surfaced then. The last line was changed to 'Then they did the kicks' if there were boys around!

> Charlie Chaplin
> Went to France
> To teach the ladies how to dance.
> First they did the cancan
> Then they did the splits,
> Then they did the okey cokey -
> Then they showed their knicks.

Bubble Car

A skipping rhyme I remember from the 60s was:

> I had a little Bubble car, number 28,
> I took it round the corner, and then I shut the gate.

Shelley Cuff,
born 1960, Chorley, toy collector

We had a slightly different version of the Bubble Car rhyme (late 60s-early 70s). Ours was:

> Bumper car, bumper car, number 28
> Haring round the cor...ner
> Your engine's out!

You skipped in for the first part, ran out on 'Haring...' back in on '...ner, Your engine's out', ran out of the rope on 'out', fast as possible, ready for the next person to take your place.

Sharon White, teaching assistant and involved with musical theatre

Coffee

One of those nonsense rhymes with dozens of variations. Its main purpose was to provide a rhythm, and skippers would often make up their own variations as they skipped. A second skipper would join in when their name was called and the original skipper would leave when they sang 'I don't like someone in with me'

> I like coffee,
> I like tea
> I like Kathy to skip with me!
> I don't like coffee,
> I don't like tea
> I don't like Diane in with me.

In hot water
Two people would be turning the rope for you and you would all chant, "I like coffee, I like tea, I like someone in with me!" Then someone else would jump in too... Then you would say, "I don't like coffee, I don't like tea, I don't like someone in with me!" and they would jump back out.

Trish Maunder, freelance art educator, mum of two

I'm trying to remember all the many skipping rhymes we had at school. One skipping rhyme I do remember was quite short and was 'I like coffee, I like tea, I like Sharon in with me!' At that point, someone would join in with the skipping. I need to keep thinking as there were so many. Another one that does spring to mind is one person holding each end of the rope and a very long line of people waiting their turn to skip in, and usually you went in and did one skip and ran out again followed in quick succession by the next person, with no gap. I think we used to say something like 'A loopy', and if we were missing one turn of the rope it was 'A loopy, miss a loop!'

Sharon White, teaching assistant and involved with musical theatre

The 'Down' rhymes

The three chants, 'Down by the Meadow', 'Down by the River' and 'Down in the Valley', are all based on the same idea of a fast ending, the skipper trying to keep up with a rope being turned faster and faster. If they get caught on the rope, they're out.

Bluebell, Cockleshell.

Down by the Meadow

> Down by the meadow
> Where the green grass grows
> There sits Susan
> Washing her clothes
> She sings a song,
> A song so sweet
> That she calls to her boyfriend
> Walking down the street
> And his name is Robert.
> Took her to the cinema
> Sat her on his knee
> Said 'Baby, will you marry me?'
> Yes – no – yes – no etc.

Wedding colours

If you didn't get through the verse or you landed on no, then you were out. If you landed on 'yes', then you went on to:

What colour wedding dress will you have? – White, black, red, see-through

What colour shoes? White, black, red, see-through

What type of house? Flat, house, bungalow, mansion

How many children? One, two, three, four

What day of the week? Monday, Tuesday, Wednesday, Thursday

This could go on indefinitely – Colour of the bridesmaid dresses, (White, black, red, see-through), How you get to the church (Car, carriage, wheelbarrow, dustcart) or When will the wedding be (This year, next year, sometime, never).

Jenna Brewer, born 1980,
ballet and bunnny enthusiast

Jump or risk bruises.

Down by the River
Everyone counts as the skipper jumps as the rope is turned faster and faster

Down by the river,
Down by the sea,
Johnny broke a bottle
And he blamed me.
I told Ma, and she told Pa
Johnny got a spanking.
Ha, ha ha
How many spanks did Johnny get?
One, two, three, four...

Down in the Valley
Like the previous game, keep counting until the skipper is out

Down in the valley
Where the green grass grows,
There sat a young girl
Picking a rose.
She sang, she sang
She sang so sweet
Along came a young man
And kissed her cheek
How many kisses did he give her?
One, two, three, four...

Dutch Girl
The Dutch Girl, Girl Guide and Fairy are very much alike, requiring similar actions such as saluting, bowing and turning around, hence the need for a long rope – the skipper can't perform these actions when they are holding the handles

I'm a little Dutch girl
Dressed in blue
Here are the things
I like to do –
Salute to the captain,
Bow to the queen,
Turn my back
On the submarine.
I can do the tap dance
I can do the splits,
I can do the okey cokey
Just like this.

Esau

Although in the 1950s, this was a hit song for the Ames Brothers, the actual rhyme – or tongue-twister – goes back much further. There are many variations, but all have the same, good, skipping beat

I saw Esau
Sitting on a see-saw
I saw Esau
With my Kate.
I saw Esau
Sitting on a see-saw
Kissing her by the garden gate.

Esau 2

I saw Esau, sitting on a see-saw,
I saw Esau, he saw me.
I saw Esau, sitting on a see-saw,
I saw Esau, he saw me.
I saw Esau, he saw me,
and she saw I saw Esau.

Esau 3

I saw Esau sitting on a see-saw,
I saw Esau kissing Kate.
But did you know that all three saw –
For I saw him
And he saw me
And Kate saw I saw Esau.

I can skip but I don't do sissy rhymes!

Halcyon days

I have memories of the long, warm summer evenings when it was Double Summertime and the day went on forever. We lived in a rural village but there was a small road of white concrete where we used to congregate in the evening because it was an ideal surface for skipping. Our long skipping rope was stretched across the width of the road and we played happily without any worries of traffic mowing us down. Perhaps there was a very occasional car but it was mostly bicycles when dads came home in the evening from the two factories three miles away. They were happy to dismount and walk on the pavement in order not to spoil our games. We would play on until one by one the mums would come out and call 'Bedtime'. What a gentle world it seemed!

Mary Rippon, enjoys gardening and antiques, Gloucestershire

Fairy

See also Dutch Girl and Girl Guide.

> *I'm a little fairy wearing blue,*
> *These are the things that I must do*
> *Curtsey to the elf who is dressed in green*
> *And blow a kiss to the fairy queen.*

Flies

A nonsense rhyme, presumably invented by a child, but which crops up in both Britain and the USA

> *Flies in the kitchen*
> *Flies in the kitchen*
> *Shoo them out*
> *Shoo them out*
> *Flies in the kitchen.*

Flu

Basically a pun, but it made a good skipping rhyme. As with all skipping games, certain precautions should be taken – skippers should ensure they wear well-fitting shoes or trainers – not loose flip flops – avoiding trailing laces or undone buckles

> *I opened the window*
> *And in flu enza,*
> *I opened the door*
> *And in come tax.*

Most young girls enjoy skipping.

Girl Guide

See also Dutch Girl and Fairy.

Girl Guides were formed by Baden-Powell in 1910, after appeals by girls who wanted something similar to the successful Boy Scout movement. Therefore, this next verse can't be earlier than 1910 but I would place it in the early 1920s. The reference to the 'boys in green' is assumed to be Scouts, although their uniform was more khaki than green (although they wore green kerchiefs). The King and Queen, presumably, were George V and Queen Mary, who reigned from 1910-1936.

> *I am a Girl Guide dressed in blue,*
> *These are the actions I must do,*
> *Salute to the King and bow to the Queen*
> *And turn around to the boys in green.*

I Had a Little Puppy

Sometimes sung as a nursery song, this skipping rhyme allows children to run in as a character is called, 'In came the doctor, in came the nurse; in came the lady with the alligator purse'

> I had a little puppy
> His name was Tiny Tim ,
> I put him in the bathtub
> To see if he could swim.
> He drank down all the water
> He ate a bar of soap,
> Soon he had a bubble in his throat -
> In came the doctor,
> In came the nurse
> In came the lady with the alligator purse.

I Had a Sausage

Sung to the tune of 'Bonnie Highland Lassie', this was probably a 1930s parody

> I had a sausage
> A bonny highland sausage
> And I put it in the cupboard for my tea.
> I went to the cellar
> To get my um-ber-ella
> And the sausage ran after me.

Jelly

There are several versions of this, but this seems the most common

> Jelly on a plate
> Jelly on a plate
> Wibble wobble
> Wibble wobble
> Jelly on a plate.

Mabel

Definitely one for doing the 'bumps' (see p131) – the 'salt, mustard, vinegar, pepper' phrase frequently crops up in children's rhymes. Here, the word 'salt' was the signal to skip in double-fast time. Keep repeating 'salt, mustard, vinegar, pepper', turning the rope faster and faster

> Mabel, Mabel, set the table
> Do it as fast as you are able,
> Don't forget the salt, mustard, vinegar, pepper.

It's fun to skip in the same rope...

...but you must make sure you both jump together.

Mickey Mouse

Mickey Mouse made his first appearance in 'Steamboat Willie' in 1928, so this rhyme can't be any older than that

> *Mickey Mouse*
> *Built a house*
> *How many bricks*
> *Did he need?*
> *One, two, three......*

Miss Polly

A rhyme often heard as a nursery song, but also used for group skipping, with children playing the parts of Miss Polly and the Doctor

> *Miss Polly had a dolly who was sick sick sick,*
> *So she told the doctor to be quick quick quick.*
> *The doctor came with his bag and his hat*
> *And he knocked on the door with a rat tat tat.*
> *He looked at the dolly and he shook his head*
> *He said 'Miss Polly, put her straight to bed.'*
> *He wrote on a paper for a pill pill pill*
> *I'll be back in the morning with my bill bill bill.*

Playing with friends
I like skipping together as well as on my own.

Lucy White, aged 6

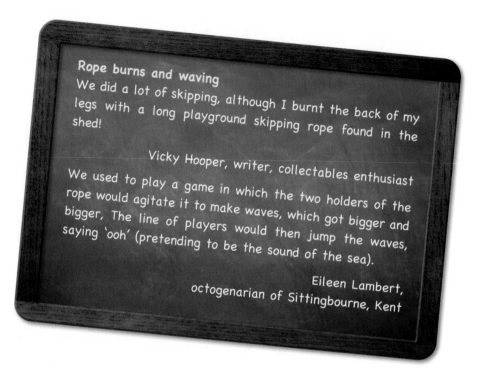

Moses

This 'Moses' chant is another child's rhyme, which seems to date back quite a long way. It was also performed by Gene Kelly and Donald O'Connor in a memorable routine in the 1952 movie, 'Singin' in The Rain'

> *Moses supposes his toeses are roses*
> *But Moses supposes erroneously.*
> *For Moses he knowses his toeses aren't roses*
> *As Moses supposes his toeses to be.*

Peter and Paul

One of those odd little rhymes which most people know and which can be acted out in skipping! Two people turn the rope, and two players run in – 'Peter' and 'Paul'. When they are named, they wave and try to avoid getting their arms caught in the rope. They run out on 'fly away' and return on 'come back'. (See also Indoor Play, Chapter 13, p169)

> *Two little dickie birds*
> *Sitting on the wall.*
> *One named Peter,*
> *One named Paul.*
> *Fly away, Peter*
> *Fly away, Paul.*
> *Come back, Peter*
> *Come back, Paul.*

Pumpkin

Based on a very old rhyme, this has been around for at least 200 years, and has been adopted as a skipping rhyme to help solo skippers keep in time with the rope

Peter, Peter pumpkin eater.
Had a wife and couldn't keep her.
Put her in a pumpkin shell
And there he kept her very well.

Rainbow colours!

We used to play a game called Rainbows. It was played with a very long skipping rope and a number of children. Everyone chose to be a different colour. The first child would run into the turning rope calling out her colour and after a short time would shout out another colour; the child who had chosen that particular colour then joined the child skipping and did exactly the same as the first child. This would continue, each new child calling a colour until all the children playing had joined the skipping and that was the Rainbow. It was all very exciting when the rope was turning and everyone jumping until someone put a foot wrong and then it had to begin again.

Mary Rippon, enjoys gardening and antiques, Gloucestershire

Rubber Dolly

An adaptation of this rhyme later became a hit in the 1960s for Shirley Ellis, as a clapping song. Here, though, it is used as a skipping chant

My mummy told me,
If I was goody
She would buy me
A rubber dolly.
My auntie told her
I kissed a soldier,
Now she won't buy me
A rubber dolly.

Sausages

A similar idea to the 'Jelly' chant, and which is often used as a second verse. It gives a good skipping rhythm

> Sausages in a pan
> Sausages in a pan
> Sizzle sizzle
> Sizzle sizzle
> Sausages in a pan.

Teddy Bear

The skipper would be expected to perform the actions sung from turning around, to touching their shoe – all without getting tangled in the rope. Probably the most favourite of the skipping rhymes, this one with all the actions, is initially quite difficult to master. The actions are listed in the song – 'touch the ground', 'turn around' 'touch a shoe' etc – and, in spite of the babyish notion of a song about a teddy bear, would even be sung by the 'big girls'!

> Teddy bear, teddy bear,
> Touch the ground.
> Teddy bear, teddy bear
> Turn around.
> Teddy bear, teddy bear
> Do the kicks.

Ready, steady, jump.

Teddy bear, teddy bear
Do the splits.
Teddy bear, teddy bear
Climb the stairs.
Teddy bear, teddy bear
Say your prayers.
Teddy bear, teddy bear
Turn out the light.
Teddy bear, teddy bear
Say goodnight.
Teddy bear, teddy bear,
Jump so high.
Teddy bear, teddy bear,
Touch the sky.
Teddy bear, teddy bear,
Touch your shoe.
Teddy bear, teddy bear,
That will do.

There's Somebody under the Bed

A fun one, which begins with one skipper, who shouts out the name of the person
she wants in the rope with her. The first skipper runs out on 'You've gotta get out'
leaving the new skipper to begin the rhyme again

There's somebody under the bed
I don't know who it is!
I feel so jolly nervous –
I call my neighbour in.
In comes Sally
Under the bed she looks –
You've gotta get out!
You've gotta get out!
There's somebody under the bed!

Vote Vote Vote

This starts with two skippers. The first one (Linda) runs out on 'won't', and a new person runs in to join the other skipper on the first 'vote' when the rhyme is repeated

> *Vote vote vote for Jenny Thompson*
> *Leaving Linda at the door.*
> *For Jenny is the one*
> *Who'll give us lots of fun*
> *And we won't vote for Linda anymore –*
> *Close the door!*

Did you know?

- Little girls of the 1850s were warned of 'instances of blood vessels burst by young ladies who, in a silly attempt to jump a certain number of hundred times, have persevered in jumping after their strength was exhausted.' ('The Girl's Own Book', 1850s)
- English folklore experts have suggested that the origins of skipping are based on the rope which was used by Judas Iscariot to hang himself after his betrayal of Christ
- Hundred Rope Jumping was one of the favourite sports during the New Year Festival held in ancient China, while exercise ropes have long been part of the Indian culture
- At one time, skipping was traditional at Easter in many villages, especially in Cambridgeshire and in Alciston, East Sussex

TYPES OF SKIPPING

Bumps
This is the fastest skipping you can do, a good 'bumper' can twirl the rope so fast that it speeds at twice the normal rate, allowing her to skip at double speed. Bumps was a form of very fast skipping, done to the rhythm of, 'salt, mustard, vinegar, pepper' (see also Mabel, p124).

Double Dutch
This is a more complicated skipping technique which involves the 'turners' turning two ropes at once, while the skipper – or sometimes skippers – attempts to jump over both ropes.

Double skipping
Played by two children sharing one standard skipping rope. The rope is held by one child, whilst the other child, facing either forwards or back, must attempt to match her skipping rhythm.

French skipping
Not really skipping as such, this is a game performed with a length of elastic stretched between the ankles of two girls, while the others jump over it in various ways. One of the chants used is

England, Ireland, Scotland, Wales
Inside, outside, inside, on!

Simplest toys are the best.

Elastic times

The elastic was the flat type, like knicker elastic and was tied to form a loop. The game needed at least three players. Two people would put the elastic around the back of their ankles and stretch it until they were a few feet apart. Then the person whose turn it was would make various manoeuvres within the elastic. One move was to jump onto both sides of the elastic and off and then jump back over, backwards, landing on both strands of elastic in turn. If you missed landing on them, you were out and took your place holding the elastic. I think that manoeuvre was called old English. Another was to stand with feet placed either side of the elastic, twist it once and then jump; the aim was to land back in the elastic. I can't remember any more moves but if you achieved them all you then tried again but this time the elastic would be moved up to the holders' knees. I know it sounds complex but once you got the hang it was a great game for little expense. We would play this game in the playground. If you had an elastic it was quite a status symbol.

Shelley Cuff, born 1960, Chorley, toy collector

In French skipping, the elastic started off round the ankles, this stage was called 'Ankles'. If you successfully got the chant and actions correct, the elastic would be moved up to the knees and you would start again. When it was around the knees it was known as 'Kneesies'.

Jenna Brewer, born 1980, ballet and bunny enthusiast

I was an only chid and even though I had tons of friends to play with all the time, I got infinite amounts of pleasure doing elastic skipping with the elastic stretched around two rubbish bins. I had to constantly move it up and down the bins as I progressed in the game but still remember, after more than 40 years, the ease and intensity of the game when played alone. One bugbear was if the bins were not full or heavy enough, they would fall over if I tripped on the rope – grrr!

Trish Maunder, freelance art educator, mum of two

Health and safety

French skipping has recently been banned in many schools, as it is feared dangerous and children might trip on the elastic.

Jump the rope

Not a skipping game as such, but played with a skipping rope and the cause of many bruised ankles. Basically, everyone forms a circle, and one child (the sensible one!) stands in the centre holding a skipping rope by one handle. She swings the rope round the circle, keeping it low to the ground, and the other players have to jump over as the rope passes. It is most effective when using a skipping rope with a heavy wooden handle...!

How high can you jump?

Bruiser
It hurt when you missed the jump, I used to get terrible bruises on my legs and ankles.

Jenna Brewer, born 1980,
ballet and bunny enthusiast

133

11. Flower Games

DAISY CHAINS

GIRLS, especially, would spend their playtimes and dinnertimes gathering daisies for chains. This, obviously, was a spring and summer pastime, and could only be undertaken if there was access to the playing field or verges, and also if the caretaker hadn't decided to cut the grass that day! Sometimes, the chains were used to make necklaces and bracelets, and often there were a dozen or so girls working on one daisy chain, aiming to see how long a chain they could make. There might even be a competition between groups. Some of the girls would be gathering the daisies, with the longest stalks they could find, while others would be threading them together, before finally linking up the chain. You needed a long finger or thumbnail to make the slot in the stalk, unless you happened to have a pin. When it was time to go back into school, the daisy chains were left wilting in the sun. Occasionally buttercups – or even, in desperation, dandelions – would be used if there were few daisies around. The caretaker used to grumble that the long chains of flowers left on the field clogged up the mower.

Do You Like Butter?
A buttercup would be picked by one child and held under a friend's chin. If there was a golden reflection on the skin, that was a sure sign they liked butter!

Grottoes
One of the more delightful games, which now seems to be obsolete, was Grottoes. Although this tended to be more of a street game than a playground pursuit – because it was often done to earn pennies – it could also be played at school, keeping small girls amused for ages. Basically, children collected pretty leaves, flowers, feathers, pebbles, stones, pieces of glass, shards of pottery and small trinkets, and created a little house or 'grotto' against a wall for others to admire.

Although Grottoes as such probably isn't now played, girls still build little creations, especially in

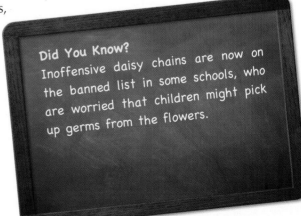

Did You Know?
Inoffensive daisy chains are now on the banned list in some schools, who are worried that children might pick up germs from the flowers.

summer on the school field, by entwining grasses and collecting pebbles. These are decorated with daisies, dandelions and buttercups and often a caterpillar or small insect is coaxed inside as an occupant.

Halfpenny hopes

We collected fine dirt from the gutter and chose a pavement slab by a wall and made a design with the dirt and then decorated [it] with flower heads, leaves and grasses. We would try our luck begging for a halfpenny.

Marjorie Last,
senior citizen, Essex

He Loves You, He Loves You Not
Long-suffering daisies could also be pressed into service as a kind of fortune-telling plant. A daisy would be picked, then the petals would be picked off one at a time to the chant of 'He loves me, he loves me not' to see if your boyfriend was true to you – or if another boy really loved you.

Lip-cutting grass
A certain variety of grass with a rough surface could be rubbed over a lip to cut it and make it bleed. It hurt, and you normally only did it the once, unless you were a masochist!

Plantain guns
Long-stemmed plantains would be picked, the stem wrapped just below the seedhead, then pulled, like a trigger. If you were lucky, the seedhead could hit your opponent, or unsuspecting victim, several feet away.

12. Playing with Things

DON'T LOSE YOUR MARBLES

CHILDREN like to take toys to school. Usually, the chosen toys are small items which fit into pockets or bags. Sometimes, they'll be the latest craze – Rubik's Cube, for example, which everyone seemed to play with in the early 1980s – but often they are 'seasonal toys', such as conkers in the autumn.

Smaller children will sometimes take in a soft toy, or maybe a doll. Dolls, sadly, don't seem so popular now, but a few decades ago, a small Rosebud or similar would be fitted into a blazer pocket ready for playtime. Often the dolls wore school uniform, too – school outfits could be obtained for most little dolls, often complete with blazers, pudding-basin felt hats and miniature satchels. In the 1970s and 80s, girls occasionally took in Barbie or Sindy dolls, but today's girls tend to be more sophisticated. When I was at infants' school in the 1950s, we were allowed to take our doll's prams to school to trundle round the playground.

Fivestones

This is an old game, which dates back to Ancient Greece, where it was referred to as Astragals. It was certainly played by the Romans, who called it Tali, and it also gained the name of Knucklebones, as the five playing pieces were commonly the knucklebones from goats or sheep. Later, knucklebone-shaped pieces were cast in materials such as glass, marble, ivory, terracotta or precious metals. Today, it is even possible to buy resin and

Hoop La!

plastic 'knucklebones'. A collection of playing pieces made from many different materials can be seen in the British Museum.

The alternative name, fivestones, became common once the game had spread, because pebbles were very easy to find and it meant that children looking for entertainment could easily find the required five small stones. Later on, shaped fivestones were sold. They were usually square clay cubes in various pastel colours, about the size of a sugar lump. Each cube was grooved. Sometimes the cubes were made from wood. Somewhere along the way, it acquired an alternative name, Dibs.

Clay fivestones are still made today.

How to play fivestones

The game of fivestones involves placing all five stones in the palm of the hand, then tossing them in the air and flipping the hand so that, hopefully, some or all of the stones land on the back of the hand. The process is then repeated.

The stones which have fallen to the ground are then picked up one by one, at the same time tossing one of the caught stones. The stones must be picked up with the catching hand. The game is then repeated by picking up two stones at time, then three, and finally, four. Various adaptations of the game include Arches, Pecks and Bushels. The popular game of Jacks evolved from fivestones.

Homemade fivestones

When the game fivestones became popular at school, we couldn't buy any so we made our own using the clay soil from the Run and baked them in the sun. They didn't last very long but the care and time that went into the making was more enjoyable than the game.

Joan Warne, children's home resident in the 1930s

I remember a game we played at school called 'fivestones'. The stones were different colours and it was played in a similar way to Jacks. The stones were smooth to touch, square in shape but had shallow grooves on the surface. This was a very popular game and groups of us used to congregate by the water fountain!

Sharon White, teaching assistant and involved with musical theatre

I played fivestones and hopscotch. I really liked fivestones and this helped tremendously when I broke a wrist a few years ago and had to do certain exercises with OXO cubes!

Edna Higgins, Hertfordshire schoolgirl in the 1940s

Jacks

This seems to be one of the most fondly-remembered games, especially by girls, from the 1950s-70s. It bears great similarities to the older game of fivestones but is played with ten, strangely-shaped, small metal playing pieces. Each piece is in the shape of a three-dimensional cross with six prongs, and each prong has a rounded end. You also need a small bouncy ball. Traditionally, the metal pieces and the ball are contained in a little cotton drawstring bag.

A set of Jacks would keep pupils amused all through playtime.

How to play Jacks

The players sit on the playground – you can't play Jacks on the school field as you can't scoop up the Jacks properly from the grass – and the game is started by each player taking it in turns to hold all the Jacks on the palm of their hand, then tossing them into the air, twisting the wrist so that the Jacks land on the back of the hand. Hopefully, one person will have caught more than the others, so they will be the 'starter' – if not, the process is repeated between those who scored the highest. Once a starter is chosen, the game can begin.

Beginning with the starter, the players take turns to throw the Jacks as before. They discard those they have managed to catch. The rest are then gathered, one at a time, by tossing the ball in the air, grabbing the Jacks and catching the ball before it bounces. Once all the players have done this, the manoeuvre is repeated, but this time the aim is to grab two Jacks and catch the ball, then three, and so on. The winner is the first to scoop all the remaining Jacks on their turn.

As with fivestones, there are many variations, and one of the reasons both of these games proved so popular was that they could be played by one player, as well as two, or even a fairly large group so were very sociable playtime games.

Marbles

This is an ancient game, and marbles made from clay or stone have been found in archaeological sites worldwide. The British Museum contains examples from Rome and ancient Egypt. Glass marbles were made in Venice, while marbles made from china were introduced around the 1800s. Marbles have been made from all

Beautiful toys – it's quite hard to find two absolutely identical marbles.

kinds of materials, including real marble, as well as nuts, bone, stone, clay, china and glass. In 1846, a German glassblower invented 'marble scissors', a tool to make glass marbles economically. Soon glass marbles of all colours and patterns were being made. Machines for manufacturing glass marbles were first introduced at the end of the Nineteenth Century. Children who couldn't afford marbles in the early Twentieth Century used to prise out the round glass stoppers used in fizzy drink bottles of the time.

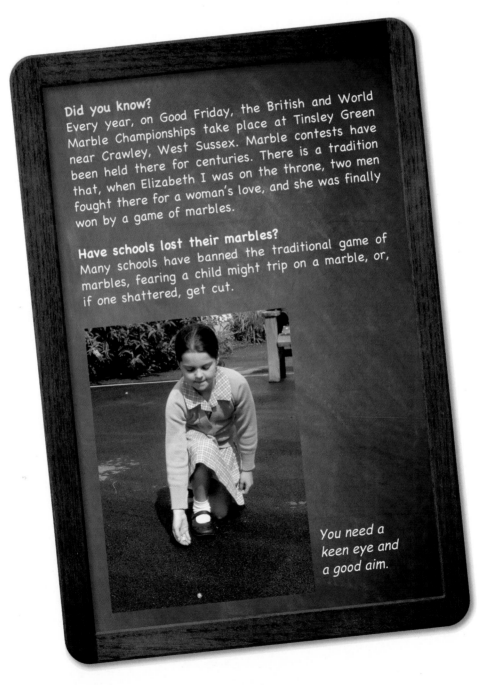

Did you know?

Every year, on Good Friday, the British and World Marble Championships take place at Tinsley Green near Crawley, West Sussex. Marble contests have been held there for centuries. There is a tradition that, when Elizabeth I was on the throne, two men fought there for a woman's love, and she was finally won by a game of marbles.

Have schools lost their marbles?

Many schools have banned the traditional game of marbles, fearing a child might trip on a marble, or, if one shattered, get cut.

You need a keen eye and a good aim.

Traditionally, in Britain, spring is the 'marble season'. There are many different games played with marbles, with the small balls being given alternative names depending on where they're played. The marble actually in use by a player is often called a taw, tolley or a shooter, while the best marbles are alleys. Most children tend to play a basic game of rolling or flicking a marble, which the next player must try to hit with their marble. If 'keepsies' is played, then the other player is allowed to keep the marble if they successfully hit it. The person who collects up the stray marbles and returns them to the players is known as the knobbler.

Yo-yo

This is another very old game, and one that is much-loved around the world. The Ancient Greeks played with yo-yos, but they are believed to have originated in China. The Greek yo-yos were made from terracotta, metal or wood, and various artefacts still survive decorated with pictures of youths playing with toys. The yo-yo consists of two small discs joined with a short spindle through the middle. A length of cord runs around the spindle and, when the end of the cord is looped around a finger, the discs can be made to travel up and down the cord.

Although the toy has such a long history, it made little impact on Western Society until the early 1930s, when a craze swept through Britain and America. A yo-yo championship was held in London which was won by a thirteen-year-old boy and, from then on, the spinning discs became well-known to children (and adults). It was such a simple toy that it could be made quickly and cheaply and was portable enough to slip in a pocket to be played with at school.

In the mid-1950s, another yo-yo craze swept the UK, and various more sophisticated models appeared, often made from colourful metal or plastic, and they whistled as they whizzed up and down the string. After yet another bout of yo-yo mania in the 1960s, things went rather quiet as toys started to become more high-tech. However, clever promotion and advertising in the 1990s put the toy firmly in the spotlight again.

With practise, many tricks can be played, including:

- Walking the Dog – *Where the yo-yo walks along the floor before being rewound*
- Rock the Baby – *The yo-yo is rocked inside a triangle formed by the string*
- Loop the Loop – *It's flicked to the front and, when it travels back, it's flicked again*
- Monkey – *It's draped over the fingers so it hangs vertically, then made to travel up and down*

Metal, wood or plastic - every one has their favourite yo-yo.

Did you know?

- In 1815, before the Battle of Waterloo, Napoleon and his army were seen relaxing by playing with yo-yos before battle.

- Yo-yos are another traditional plaything which have been banned in many schools on 'health and safety grounds' as they can give users black eyes or be used to trip up others.

Diabolo

Yet another ancient pastime, it is believed that this game originated in China at least 4,000 years ago and, even today the original, bamboo diabolos are made there, with holes in the sides to make them whistle as they are spun. Basically, a diabolo consists of two cones joined together which are rocked, thrown or spun on a cord suspended from two sticks. One stick is held in each hand. However, the early diabolos were cylindrical and, sometimes, very large.

Later, the game was introduced to Europe, becoming very fashionable in early Nineteenth Century France, but the toy was a globular shape, resembling a dumbbell. In the early Twentieth Century, a French engineer developed the toy, refining the shape until it resembled the two cones we know today. It became so popular that people soon developed all kinds of tricks, and at various times over the Twentieth Century the diabolo has appeared as a craze amongst school children. The 1980s saw a revival, thanks to modern materials and fine-tuning which allowed the performance of many more tricks and, these days, it is often used as part of a juggling act. The down side of taking a diabolo to school is, unlike the yo-yo, a diabolo isn't so easy to carry around because of the two unwieldy sticks.

Hoop rolling

Hoops are a traditional toy. For centuries, children have played with a hoop constructed from reed, willow or vine. Often, though, these were bowled, thrown or skipped with, rather than spun around the waist using the 'hula' hip movement. In Victorian and Edwardian times, bowling a hoop was one of the most popular games, and children across England would chase after a wooden or metal hoop using a stick to guide it along and is depicted as one of the archetypal childhood images of this time.

Thin wooden hoops for twirling are used at school for gymnastics, and, of course, the late fifties saw the hula-hoop craze.

Victorian children playing diabolo.

However the 'bowling a hoop with a stick' games appear to have more or less fizzled out by the beginning of the First World War, though they still can be found in a few places today. Some countries, including America and China, still hold hoop races and competitions.

Hoop bowling is a very old sport; we know that because pictures of young men bowling their hoops appear on vases from Ancient Greece. Later hoops were made of wood or metal, from old barrels or from wheels, and the skill was to see how long the hoop could be kept rolling when guided just by a stick. Victorian shops selling toys often sold purpose-made wooden hoops and the sticks for bowling them along.

Hula-hoop

The major hula-hoop craze began in the late 1950s, when an American company called Wham-O developed a hoop made of a new kind of plastic, Marlex. In 1958, over twenty million were sold. The impact of this toy was huge, especially with young teens and, for a while throughout Britain, everyone, it seemed, was gyrating their hips while spinning the hoop. Hula-hoop competitions were held, and it was even incorporated into various dances. Although not easily portable (nowadays, hoops are more easily carried as collapsible ones are available), during the main 1950s craze, children lugged their hula-hoops to school to practise in the playground. The hula-hoop was the first major teen fad, arguably the one responsible for bringing this age group to the attention of manufacturers, who suddenly realised that teenagers were a consumer group to be recognised in their own right; an untapped, primary market.

I remember my father buying me a hula-hoop as a surprise. It was large, made from ribbed yellow plastic, and he carried it home over one shoulder, while riding his bicycle! Hoops, of course, are a standard piece of school equipment, used in many games. They can be used for skipping, as 'islands' for jumping in and out of, for spinning around arms and legs, for crawling through, and much more besides. When I was at school, they were usually made of bent

Twist the waist...

...bend the knees.

wooden strips, and could give your ankles a painful clip if you weren't careful when you skipped with them. These days, many hoops are made of plastic.

Spinning a hoop.

Looperoo
Using a rope like a lasso, children whirled the loop in the air, in front of themselves and around their body. This seems to be an earlier version of the 1950s 'cowboy lasso' much beloved of small boys at the time. Needless to say, a lasso being thrown around during playtime would be a health and safety risk today – they were even banned from our school playground in the Fifties!

Scoubidou
Scoubidou first became a fad in the early 1960s. It originated in France, a very simple toy which basically consisted of long flexible narrow plastic cords which could be knotted or woven together to form multicoloured lengths used to create bracelets, key fobs etc. As it was quick to master and fitted easily into a pocket, this was another perfect pursuit for school playtime, and, just as happened with Jacks, groups of girls could be seen seated on the playground as they industriously knotted their scoubidous. The craze later reappeared a few years ago; a cheap, portable pastime – but now the plastic was updated to incorporate glitter, stripes or fluorescent colours.

Once the basic knotting techniques have been mastered, attractive results can be obtained. The trick is to master the tension so that every knot is even. The easiest way to begin with scoubidou is to make a flat knot with one strand around a pencil, before threading another, different coloured, strand through the knot. Four lengths will be created, which are then knotted in turn until gradually, as the cable grows, a geometric pattern is formed. More advanced techniques include increasing the number of strands used, or making extra loops to create a round cable.

Cigarette cards
Cigarette cards were first used in the late Nineteenth Century by Allen & Ginter in the US and by W.D. and H.O. Wills in Britain. They printed designs such as sets of actresses or sports stars on the stiffeners used in cigarette packets to prevent the contents from being crushed. By the early 1900s, school children had realised that here was a ready-made game or collectable, which could be obtained 'for free' from friends or relatives who smoked. The colourful cards were traded in the school playground so that complete sets could be formed. However, many children, especially boys, used the cards in various games. The most common was to flick them against a section of cards leaning against a wall, and any that were knocked down were allowed to be kept. Another version saw them flicked against the wall and the thrower whose card was nearest was allowed to keep all the other cards.

Later, when cards used to appear in packets of tea, such as Brooke Bond and Hornimans, these cards would be used for similar games. Cards could also be found in packs of bubblegum, sweets and sweet cigarettes. Some children did actually collect the cards and stick them in the proper albums, but it wasn't so much fun…

Card games
The most popular was 'up the wall'. You flicked your card towards a wall to get as close to it as possible. The nearest took the cards. Or, if you landed on top of your opponent's card you took it. There were many more variations of this game.

Barry Carter, retired publican, Bethnal Green

Cup and ball

Cup and ball was played in the Sixteenth Century and influenced later games such as biff bat and ball and cone. It consists of a small wooden cup mounted on a handle, with a small ball attached by a string. The aim is to catch the ball in the cup, but it takes quite a lot of skill and practice to do this successfully, though the shorter the string, the easier it is to catch the ball. This traditional game must have been played in schools for centuries and, whilst still available today, is perhaps not as popular as it once was. An early variation had a hole in the ball, which was then caught on a spike rather than in a cup, while a Seventeenth Century version had a long handle at right-angles, making the cup resemble a clay pipe, rather than the more commonly-found design with a vertical handle.

According to the Toypost Company, who manufacture wooden novelties, yet another version, known as the Bilboquet or Bilbo Catch, which has a spike at one end and a cup at the other – giving the player a choice of method – was believed to have been very popular in Tudor Times. The French King Henri III was supposed to be addicted to it, while the Inuit people carved the toys out of bone.

Did you know?
Jane Austen excelled at cup and ball, according to a quote at Chawton Cottage, Hampshire, once her home and now a museum dedicated to the popular author.

Ball and cone

A plastic cone with mesh sides, it contains a powerful metal spring which is activated by a trigger at the side of the cone. A small celluloid or plastic ball is placed into the cone and, when the trigger is pulled, the ball is fired into the air. The aim is to catch it again in the cone, which is not as easy as it sounds. Once the game has been mastered, enthusiasts try to fire and catch two balls at once. This is another toy which found popularity in the 1950s, and tends to appear from time to time, as it's not too heavy to store in a school bag. I used to play with one of these toys for hours: the difficulty was the co-ordination, as it was necessary to throw your head back to keep an eye on the ball, attempt to position the cone under the ball as it fell, run backwards to make sure you were in the right place – and normally be dazzled by the sun shining straight into your eyes. To make things worse, invariably the ball bounced out of the cone again instead of being trapped inside.

Ball and cone, a rather frustrating toy.

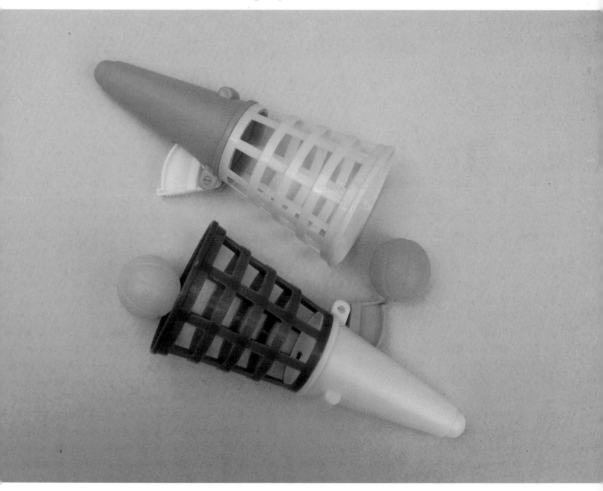

Biff bat

A basic, easy-to-find toy, the biff bat is a simple idea which, like other similar toys, goes in and out of fashion. It was popular in the late 1930s, again in the fifties, and reappeared in the 1980s. The biff bat consists of a round wooden bat with a small rubber ball fastened to the centre by a length of elastic. The idea is to hit the ball with the bat and keep hitting – or biffing – it for as long as possible. My father used to fashion these toys from a piece of plywood, sandpapering it smooth and then attaching a small rubber ball in which he had drilled a hole to thread the elastic. Nowadays, the bats are often made from plastic, or designed as a small tennis racquet with a mesh grid.

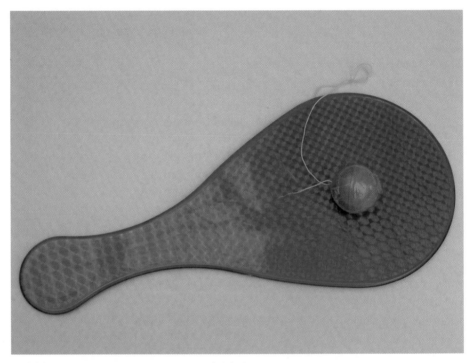

Biff bat – not quite as easy as it looks.

Whip and top

Another old game, the whip and top seems to have become almost forgotten now but it was very popular in the 1930s. It consists of a small wooden top and a length of cord or leather thong which is wrapped around the top, then pulled sharply to make the top spin. Apparently, whip-tops were known in ancient cultures in China, Egypt, Greece and Rome, and were played with not only by children but by adults, too. Throwing tops are slightly more recent, and are started off with the cord before being thrown and left to spin. There are many different kinds of tops, but the whip and top is probably the one which appeared in most school playgrounds, as it could be whipped and coaxed along the ground and used to race against others.

Racing blue
After making patterns on the top with chalk, the tops were known as 'Window-breaker'. I wonder why?!!

Eileen Lambert, octogenarian of Sittingbourne, Kent

In April, our tops were painted either Oxford or Cambridge blue, and our whips were carefully chosen through trial and error to be just the right length and texture; an old bootlace giving the best results. So we had our own 'boat-race' contest, whipping the tops from one end of the playground to the other to the cheers of our supporters.

Joan Warne, children's home resident in the 1930s

1930s Boat Race doll

Ankle skip ball

Popular in the 1960s, the ankle skip ball reappeared in a more sophisticated form in the late 1980s. A plastic hoop fitted around one ankle and had a string attached; sometimes the hoop was omitted and the string was looped around the ankle. A ball was fixed to the string and the object of the game was to swing the ball around the leg while jumping over the string. It could be played either on the spot, or moving forward. Later versions came with a counter, to make it easier to keep score.

Whizzers

Whizzers are quick and easy to make, and very satisfying. At their simplest, they consist of a disc of coloured cardboard about four inches in diameter. Two holes are punched into the centre of the disc and a length of cord is threaded through to make a loop. The player holds the loop in each hand and turns the disc round and round till the cord is twisted. Then with gentle pulls on the cord, the disc can be spun faster and faster, often making a buzzing sound and causing a kaleidoscope effect with its colourful decorations.

Cap rockets

The lethal 'Cap Rockets' were soon banned in school playgrounds in the Fifties. The metal, rocket-shaped toys in which 'caps' (sold in a roll for a penny and looking like little black blobs, intended for use in cap guns to make them bang) were fitted. These rockets were then thrown into the air, falling to earth with a satisfying bang (especially when several caps were inserted at once!) They also caused a fair amount of head injuries in our school playground!

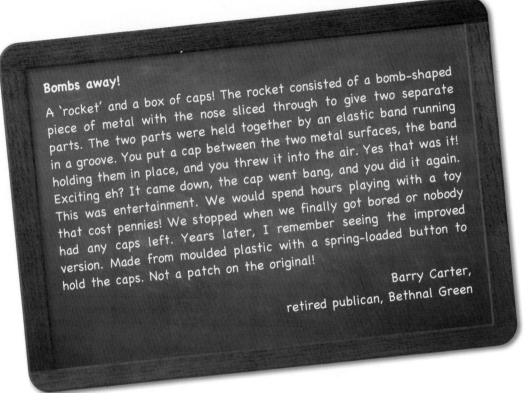

Bombs away!

A 'rocket' and a box of caps! The rocket consisted of a bomb-shaped piece of metal with the nose sliced through to give two separate parts. The two parts were held together by an elastic band running in a groove. You put a cap between the two metal surfaces, the band holding them in place, and you threw it into the air. Yes that was it! Exciting eh? It came down, the cap went bang, and you did it again. This was entertainment. We would spend hours playing with a toy that cost pennies! We stopped when we finally got bored or nobody had any caps left. Years later, I remember seeing the improved version. Made from moulded plastic with a spring-loaded button to hold the caps. Not a patch on the original!

Barry Carter,
retired publican, Bethnal Green

Conkers

This is one of those traditional, seasonal games which has been played for centuries, the rules passed down through the generations. It is free, simple to learn yet, at the same time, needs a fair amount of skill and judgement to be played successfully.

A conker is the fruit of the horse chestnut tree, and is found inside the prickly casing which falls to the ground when ripe (or when hit by a stick hurled into the tree by an impatient child). Horse chestnut trees were first introduced into Britain in the late Sixteenth Century, but the fruits weren't used to play with until around the late 1700s. Before that date, children played a similar game using various nuts such as hazel.

The selection of the conker is important; it should be firm, symmetrical, and, of course, should not have any cracks or chips. A hole needs to be drilled through the centre of the conker, using a bradawl, skewer or similar, and it is then threaded onto a length of string, about 10-12in (25-30cm) long. One person wraps the string of a conker around their hand, letting the conker hang down. The opponent, also

with a conker string wrapped around their hand, pulls back their conker before releasing it and trying to strike the hanging conker. If they miss, they're allowed two further goes, and if the strings become tangled, whoever calls 'Strings!' first, can have an extra go.

The players take turns to strike at each other's conkers, until one of the conkers is completely destroyed. Then the complicated – but highly important – scoring ritual takes over. The winning conker, assuming it has not been used in a contest before, and assuming the beaten conker was also a new one, becomes a 'one-er'. However, if the beaten conker had already beaten other conkers, the winning conker is awarded those scores as well, thus becoming perhaps a four-er, six-er or whatever.

Various methods can be used to harden a conker, to produce a champion. It can be soaked in vinegar, baked in an oven, coated in varnish – or you could use a conker from a previous year, which will have dried and hardened. In official conker championships, this kind of thing is not allowed, and fresh conkers are provided by the organisers.

Did you know?

- The World Conker Championships, first held in 1965, take place every October in Ashton, Northamptonshire. Each game lasts five minutes. The final winner is taken to the conker throne and crowned with conkers.

- Many schools have recently banned the game of conkers, fearing shards of shell might injure a child or they'll get sued over black eyes. Some schools still allow conker battles to be fought – but only if the players wear protective goggles.

Courtesy of Ashton Conker Club.

Rubik's Cube

This phenomenon, which first appeared in 1980, was ubiquitous in most school playgrounds. Children were addicted to the brightly coloured squares as they grappled to sort the colours. Some children became so proficient that they could solve it within minutes, but the majority became dispirited by being unable to master the technicalities. Later, various other versions of the 'cube' appeared, including Rubik's Magic (a flat puzzle featuring eight tiles decorated with coloured linking rings), but although popular, they weren't such a must-have.

Rubik's Cube was invented by Erno Rubik, a Hungarian sculptor and professor of architecture, in 1974, though not released worldwide until 1980. In 1980 and 1981, it won the British Association of Toy Retailers' Toy of the Year award at the British International Toy Fair. The original cube has nine square faces on each side, giving a total of fifty-four squares. Each face is covered with coloured stickers, a different colour for each side of the cube. Typically, the colours are red, blue, green, yellow, white and orange. The sides must be mixed up, then unscrambled to leave each side of the cube a solid colour. During the cube's heyday, various solutions were published, while it was not unknown for people to become so frustrated that they would dismantle the cube and rebuild it as a solved puzzle, or peel off all the coloured stickers and re-stick them in the correct places. In fact, it was even possible to buy sheets of stickers to fix over the mixed-up coloured squares, so it regained the original appearance.

Easy peasy or a major dilemma?

Complicated cube

I was useless – my dream was to complete the puzzle but I was never able to do it.

Tracy Martin,
collectables nut, cruise lecturer and
journalist

Cereal freebies

Not really a game but an important ingredient of playground play, the free gifts found in cereal packets, sweet bags, tea packets, comics and the like are a basic form of children's 'currency', to be swapped and bartered. Other things, such as cheap toys, fast food gifts, party gifts and cracker novelties also come under this heading, as do trading cards and stickers.

Usually they change hands as children attempt to build up entire sets or to complete albums. Values are set – a common item is obviously not worth as much as a rare one, so often a top card or toy is worth a dozen or more of a lesser one. Years ago, when children collected postage stamps to stick in albums, or matchbox or cheese labels, these items were traded just as fiercely. Currently, it is more likely to be Slammers, Pogs (round milk-bottle top sized discs printed with various logos or designs) or trading cards which are swapped.

An Amanda Jane doll all ready for school.

Fun in the sun.

Modern crazes

Nowadays, there is so much input from films, television and the media, as well as from manufacturers who have deliberately aimed to develop new must-have products, that it is difficult to keep up. Children will begin collecting the latest trend, only to discover a few weeks later that it is now outdated and has been superseded by something else. Pokemon trading cards (based on a Japanese cartoon) were a huge craze for a while, though many schools eventually issued a ban because, as all the cards had different values, there were problems with theft and bullying as some children were stealing the more desirable cards from their classmates. This was even more upsetting as many of the youngsters had saved a lot of pocket money to buy these special, shiny versions of the cards.

Perfect for juggling, throwing - or for stuffing a couple up your jumper as instant 'bosoms'.

Colourful currency

A big thing in the late sixties was swapping beads. Every girl had a box with different coloured beads in it, all with different values. You would swap, say, a very decorative one for three plainer ones. What the point of it was, I have no idea but it was a big thing at the time.

Catriona Macleay, age 45, Essex

Supervised play

Sometimes a keen teacher (usually one new to the profession!) would decide as an act of benevolence, or maybe just wishing to escape the staff room fug in the days before the smoking ban, to supervise a lunchtime game. Often, this would be an organised game of cricket, rounders, netball or football, or perhaps tennis practice. If we were lucky, it was an extra swimming lesson. Occasionally, it was use of the gym – using the ropes and wallbars usually, which were perfect for playing shipwrecks. When we were one of the lucky schools to be given a trampoline, some of the PE teachers sacrificed their break to allow children to experience the fun of jumping and bouncing. Safety procedures weren't as strict as they are today – I recall that several children were allowed on the trampoline at once, which could have been dangerous as the trampoline wasn't huge. On the whole though, children were left to make their own amusements, supervised by one or two staff whose turn it was to be on 'playground duty'.

Balancing, climbing or just having fun – that's what playtime is all about.

Playground games

I played marbles and had quite a stack of various sets of cigarette cards that we played flick with against the wall. At the right season, conkers too were an annual feature in the playground. None of this prevention for safety reasons. I also brought in my American comics to exchange for others or to sell. I must have run about a bit as I recall crashing my head onto another boy and being sent home with an egg-sized lump above my right eye and a fat bandage around my head like a turban! My Mother practically fainted when I walked in. I was five and was sent home unescorted – a walk of about twenty minutes. It's a wonder I'm alive. I could have been kidnapped!

Mark Wynter,

actor, singer, tearaway schoolkid

13. Indoor Play

THE SUN HAS GOT HIS MAC ON

PLAYTIME on rainy days always began with a brawl and the sound of raised voices. It wasn't the pupils, it was the staff, arguing amongst themselves as to whose turn it was to go on dreaded 'Indoor Play Duty'.

Unlike outdoor playtime, classes were not allowed to mingle, so it was annoying if your best friend was in a different class from you. Even if a teacher did take pity on you, and allowed you into your friend's class, you didn't stay there for long. It was like going into alien territory, and though you might know the names of the other children, it still felt disorientating to be in the wrong classroom.

'Rainy Day Playtime' was necessarily more circumspect than outdoor playtime – you were forbidden to run or jump or shout, for example. You couldn't throw a ball or play with a skipping rope either, and you couldn't even try to circle the room by climbing across desks and chairs without touching the floor. All of these things were definitely NOT ALLOWED! However, you were allowed to use the board games and puzzles in the cupboard, or you could play with Plasticine, draw or read. At my infants' school, a special wet day treat was to be allowed to play with a set of metal zoo animals – I was always specially taken with monkey up the palm tree!

Rainy days were loathed by the staff.

BOARD GAMES

There was a splendid, old wooden solitaire board with marbles for pegs in the 'Wet Weather' cupboard. It really made you feel you were playing an important game as you 'jumped' the marbles, carefully putting each one in the groove around the edge as you removed them from the board. The cupboard also contained a selection of board games, all the old favourites – Snakes and Ladders, Ludo, draughts, chess – and a heap of tatty jigsaw puzzles, which no one ever did as they

Board games never go out of fashion.

were too big to do in the lunch hour. Many of the boxes were split or broken, and the cupboard floor was littered with bits of puzzle, assorted counters and a few dice.

There was a ritual for throwing dice, and everyone had their own favourite method to 'ensure' they threw a lucky six, or whatever number they needed. Some children would spend a minute or so shaking the eggcup, or wooden 'shaker', others whispered endearments to the dice, or blew on the die for luck. Then there were those who put the die into the shaker and tipped it straight out (a bit of a cheat this, because you could influence the result) and those who 'accidentally' dropped the die on the floor, quickly picking it up before the other players could see the result, so they had to believe the player when they stated they had a six. Others spurned the shaker, instead holding the die in their cupped hands to 'warm it for luck' as they jiggled their hands.

Chess
This was played during lunchtimes – schools often had chess clubs, and the games could be carried over if necessary, as chess isn't really a game you can rush. Its history is shrouded in mystery, with many people believing it to be derived from a game played in India in the Sixth Century. However, another school of thought says that it's a Chinese game.

The game as we know it today probably evolved in Europe around the Fifteenth Century and, in 1849, John Jaques (see Happy Families, p165) created a new design which he based on the Elgin marbles, setting a benchmark for the pieces, easily distinguishing the king and queen from the common pawns. These famous pieces were endorsed by Englishman Howard Staunton, the world's greatest chess master. Since then, these 'Staunton sets' are the standard, and are used in tournaments worldwide.

The idea is to conquer the other player's king (checkmate), despite the king being one of the most limited pieces on the board in terms of movement. It is a game of skill requiring forethought and strategy.

Draughts

Draughts is another ancient game, and early forms of a similar game called Alquerque have been found in Egypt dating from 600BC. Nowadays, we normally play on a board eight squares by eight squares, but most of Europe uses a ten squares by ten squares format and play a slightly different form of the game. In some parts of Asia, they use boards with twelve squares down each side.

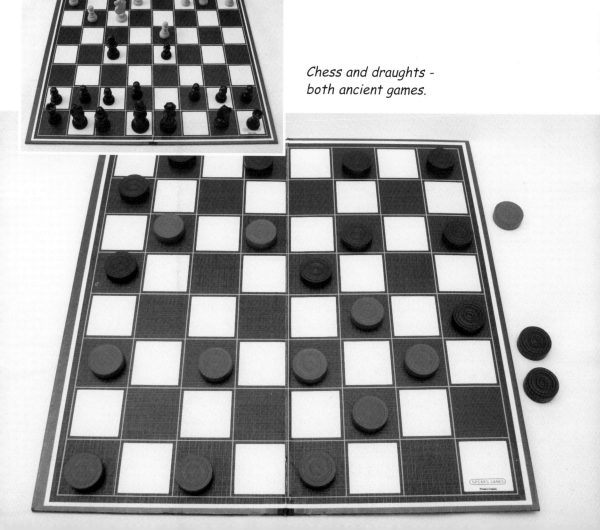

Chess and draughts - both ancient games.

Ludo

This was very popular, although everyone wanted to be red, and no one liked the green counters which were considered unlucky. Ludo is based on another Indian game, Pachisi, which was introduced into England in the 1860s. Pachisi is played with cowrie shells and is a rather complicated game needing both skill and luck. Its name is based on the Hindi word pachis, meaning 25 as that is the highest score which can be gained when playing with cowrie shells. It has been played in India in some form since 4AD and has been called 'India's national game'. Ludo is much simpler, and, apart from the board, you just need a die and some counters. Usually the board is based on a cross design with a square in each corner, and the object is to race your four counters around the board until you get them 'home' to the safety of the corner squares.

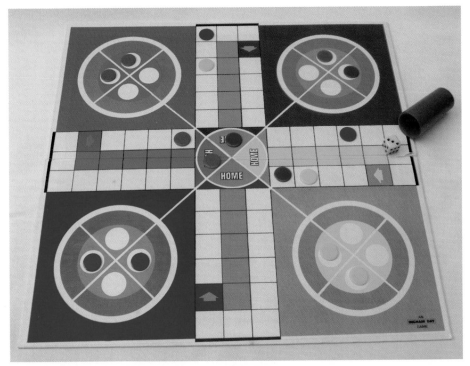

Ludo – one of the most popular board games.

Nine Men's Morris

This is one of the oldest board games known. It was played by the Ancient Greeks and the Romans and boards very similar to those used today have been found during archaeological digs. Apparently, at one time, Nine Men's Morris was played using pebbles on village greens, the board marked out in the turf, and it was also played in the wayside taverns. It even gets a mention in Shakespeare (*A Midsummer Night's Dream*, Act 2, Scene 1), 'The Nine Men's Morris is filled up with mud.' Presumably, it was raining and the village green was soaked!

Snakes and Ladders

Always a favourite, the rules were understood by the dimmest child – you threw the die (or dice as we always called it, even though the singular should be die), moving your counter along the squares, going up the ladders and down the snakes. Eventually, when the game began to pall, you reversed the rules and went up the snakes and down the ladders. Apparently, Snakes and Ladders, like many of the games we enjoy today, originated in India, and was a game used for religious instruction, teaching about vices and virtues. Virtuous acts, or ladders, shortened the journey made by the soul because it could reach Heaven more quickly. However, snakes meant reincarnation in a lower, animal form. Snakes and Ladders has been played

The colourful designs on the Snakes and Ladders' board add extra enjoyment to the game.

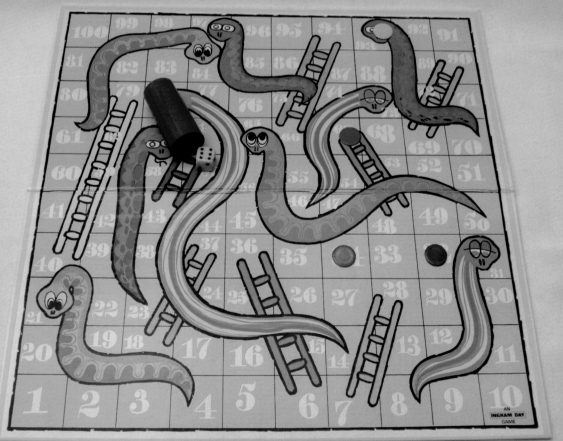

in Britain for well over a century, and the boards vary from simplistic ones for small children to attractive works of art, with the snakes beautifully decorated.

Solitaire
There was a craze for Solitaire in the late 1950s; many people acquired small portable plastic solitaire games, which came in a round compact-type of box containing the plastic board and a set of tiny white pegs. These were ideal for rainy day play, as well as for using in the playground when you just wanted to sit in peace.

A slightly more sophisticated version of the portable solitaire game.

CARD GAMES

Card games such as Snap, Beat Your Neighbour, Donkey and Happy Families were allowed – though the authorities would have punished anyone if they were caught playing poker (especially strip poker!).

Beat Your Neighbour

Often known as Beggar My Neighbour, it is also known as Beat Your Neighbour Out of Doors, Draw the Well Dry, Beat Jack Out of Doors and even Strip Jack Naked, this can be played with a standard pack of cards (52 in the set), though children normally play with a special set of 36 cards featuring various designs. Amongst them are a few 'Put' cards, which instruct the player to put down one, two or three cards. The cards are dealt to the players and they take turns to place their cards in a pile. If a Put card is turned up, the next player must put the stated number of cards on the pile. The player who put down the Put card takes all the cards in the pile, and the winner is the player with all the cards. This has been played in Britain since the 1860s, and was mentioned by Charles Dickens in his 1861 novel, *Great Expectations* when Pip played the game.

Even if you can't play the game, you can admire the artwork.

Donkey

Very similar to Old Maid but with a Donkey card, this is played with 35 cards, dealt amongst the players who remove any pairs, placing them face down on the table. They then offer their remaining cards face down to the next player, who takes one. If it matches one they already hold, they place the pair face down. When all a player's cards are paired, they are out of the game. The person with the Donkey is the loser. This type of card game is known as a 'scapegoat' game because one card is a 'losing' or scapegoat card.

Happy Families

Perhaps the most interesting of the children's card games is Happy Families, which is usually attributed to John Jaques & Son Ltd, of London, a well-known Nineteenth Century maker and publisher of games. The aim of the game is to collect complete sets of cards by taking turns to request them from other players. The characters, such as Mr Bun the Baker, Mr Bones the Butcher, Mr Bung the Brewer and Mr Tape the Tailor were originally drawn by Sir John Tenniel, best known for his illustrations in the book *Alice in Wonderland* by Lewis Carroll. A player, when asked for a specific character must give it up if they have it amongst their cards. However, if they don't have that card, they reply, "Not at home". The winner is the person who has collected the most families. One pack design, still available today, bears the legend, 'First published before the Great Exhibition 1851' as the cards were produced in time for the famous event.

A traditional Jaques set of happy families.

House of Cards
A little patience and no draughts were required to create a house of cards from a simple structure to an impressive but unstable tower block or mansion. All it took was a steady hand – and no slamming doors.

Snap

Probably the first card game most children play, it's basically a card recognition game, with players calling out "Snap" when two cards are turned up with the same design. Snap was introduced by Londoner John Jaques (see Happy Families), using similar illustrations to his Happy Families games. This is a quick and easy rainy day pastime, though it can get quite raucous!

Old Maid

This can be played with a standard set of playing cards with the Queen of Spades representing the Old Maid, though normally children use a special set consisting of matching pairs plus a single Old Maid card. After the cards are dealt, each player in turn offers the cards to the next player, face down. The player takes a card and, if it makes up a pair with one they already hold, discards them. They then offer their cards to their neighbour and so on. Eventually, one card will be left – the Old Maid – and the holder is the loser.

PAPER AND PENCIL GAMES

Many of these pencil and paper games were played not only in wet indoor playtimes but also outside.

Paper and pencils keep children amused for hours.

Alphabet games

This is basically a list-making game. You were given a letter of the alphabet and had to list a country, flower, sport, film star, animal, bird and town. There were several variations, sometimes you just had one subject and had to list as many names as you could beginning with the one letter. Another version (which took a lot longer) entailed writing out the alphabet, then thinking of words in the above categories beginning with each letter.

Battleships

Two people draw two grids, each of 100 squares (or other agreed size), or they use pieces of graph paper, then write the letters A-J across the top of the grid, and the numbers 1-10 down the side, to make a 'map reference'. Then each of them marks out the ships on one of their grids without letting the other player see. The fleet consists of:

> 1 battleship – 5 squares
>
> 2 cruisers – 4 squares
>
> 3 frigates – 3 squares
>
> 4 minesweepers – 2 squares
>
> 5 submarines – 1 square

Defensive Grid

	A	B	C	D	E	F	G	H	I	J
1										
2										
3										
4										
5										
6										
7										
8										
9										
10										

Offensive Grid

	A	B	C	D	E	F	G	H	I	J
1										
2										
3										
4										
5										
6										
7										
8										
9										
10										

These ships can be vertical or horizontal but not diagonal, and they can only touch at one corner. The makeup of the fleet can vary, it doesn't matter as long as both players agree. The first player 'fires a shell' by calling out a grid reference. If it corresponds with a ship, then the other player will call 'Hit', though won't say what kind of ship they have hit, and then marks the grid with a cross for a hit, a dot for a miss. The caller will also mark a cross for a hit and a dot for a miss on their spare grid, to enable them to keep track of the squares they have already played. If a player gets a hit, they have another go and, if successful, yet another, and so on until they have sunk the ship. This is a good game, but does take a bit of planning. Nowadays, you can get handheld battleship games – some of which have sound effects! The Battleship paper grid game predates the First World War.

Consequences

Everyone writes a girl's name on a separate piece of paper; they fold it down and pass it on to the next person. As the papers make their rounds, a boy's name is added, then where they met, what they said, where they went, and, finally, the consequence. Though sometimes these turned out to be really rude, many were very amusing, with imaginations soaring as they sent this couple on strange adventures and it was a good way to pass a playtime.

Dickie Birds

This was a clever 'conjuring' trick, and once we had discovered the secret, we never gave the game away – it was up to the puzzled watchers to guess how it was done. Until now! A child would stick a small piece of paper to both their forefingers – usually with spit – and then sit at a desk. As they recited the poem, they would lift up one finger to show 'Peter' and then the other to show 'Paul'. When the birds flew away, the forefinger was held in the air, then as it was lowered to the desk, quickly substituted for the finger next to it (which had no paper). So, by the time the player had told Paul to fly away, they had two bare fingers on the desk – the paper had magically vanished. On the cry of "Come back Peter", the finger was held up and, as it reached the desk, switched for the index finger again, and the same was done for Paul. At the end of the chant, the two paper birds were back. Very simple – but baffling if you didn't know how it was done!

> *Two little dickie birds sitting on the wall,*
> *One named Peter, one named Paul.*
> *Fly away Peter, fly away Paul,*
> *Come back Peter, come back Paul.*

Funny People

I remember playing this when I was very small, taught by my parents. When I started school, I passed it on, and it soon spread around. All you needed was a sheet of paper and a pencil. The first person would draw a head, curving their hand around the paper so the others couldn't see. They would then draw the neck, and fold the paper over so that just the neck showed. The next person would draw the arms and body, again in secret, adding lines to show where the legs should be. The last person would draw the legs and feet. Then the paper was handed to the first person to open – some of the creations were very funny, especially if imaginative animal heads or bodies were drawn.

Guess What?

This was a similar idea to Funny People, with one person drawing a section of a picture, then folding it over with a few clue lines showing. The next person did a bit more and so on. Another version was to write a sentence or two, aiming to leave the final two words showing, so that someone else could add a few more words.

Hangman

This word game for two players begins with one person thinking of a word – not too long – and writing down a dash for each letter. The second player calls out a letter and, if it is in the word, the first player writes it in, (wherever it occurs if the letter is repeated). If it isn't, then they draw the upright of a gallows. The game continues, and for each correct guess, the letter is filled in above the dash. For each wrong letter, another part of the gallows is drawn. Eventually, if the word isn't guessed, the first player will have drawn a gallows complete with a hanging stick figure. This game was played in late-Victorian times. There are now computerised versions of this playground favourite.

Noughts and Crosses

A gloriously simple game, learnt in a few seconds and never forgotten; however, once the basic strategies are mastered, most games end in a draw! Also called Tic-tac-toe, hugs and kisses or Xs and Os, amongst other things, it consists of a 3 x 3 grid. The players, one O and the other X, take turns to put their mark in a grid. The winner is the one whose symbols form a row, be it vertical, horizontal or diagonal.

Pocket-sized wooden versions of noughts and crosses are available, with pegs marked with the symbols. Using one of these saves the necessity of a paper pad and pencil!

Simple and quick to play.

Squares or Dots and Boxes

A grid is drawn out using dots, and two players take it in turns to draw a vertical or horizontal line from any dot to the next. The aim is to create a box. Each time a box is completed, the winner enters their initial and has another turn. The winner is the one who has completed the most boxes.

Origami

Origami is the art of paper folding. The word is Japanese, and its meaning is to fold (*oru*) paper (*kami*). Usually, the paper used is rectangular and it is folded without cutting. Only a few different types of folds are used, such as 'valley' (like a V) or 'mountain' (like an ^), but hundreds of animals, birds and other items can be created.

Obviously, paper was an everyday part of school life, and so it was readily available in the classroom. No one minded if we took small pieces into the playground to use for the various folding toys, or used some to make cards and decorations – another favourite pastime on wet days.

Darts and aeroplanes

Paper folding was quite popular when I was at school in the 1960s, nothing intricate but most of us could fashion a paper boat, hat or aeroplane from a sheet of notepaper. Aeroplanes and paper darts were good fun in the playground, quick and inexpensive to make. There were many designs, but the basic dart was made

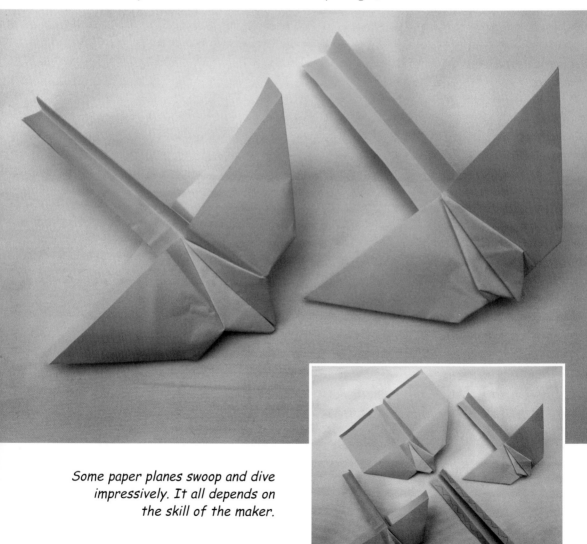

Some paper planes swoop and dive impressively. It all depends on the skill of the maker.

172

by folding a sheet of paper in half, then the corners at one end were folded in to form a point. Finally, the two folded sides were folded down again.

Paper aeroplanes were great favourites – they still are, even in this sophisticated age. There are dozens of different ways to make them, and every child has their own favourite method. I was taught how to make a paper plane by my dad when I was very small, and it was the method he learnt as a child in the 1920s – presumably, his father taught him. You began with a rectangular sheet of paper and folded it corner to corner, making a square. The extra, leftover, strip of paper at the edge was removed to make the tail. But you weren't allowed to use scissors – the strip had to be creased and folded just so, then torn. Using scissors was a namby-pamby way of doing it! I always managed fine until I got to the pinch pleat of paper on the fuselage; I never could get that bit right, and would always have to ask dad to help me, watching as his deft fingers folded the paper until he had made a neat point or 'nose' at the front. The planes flew well, and were brilliant for somersaulting – paper planes, paper darts and paper gliders were allowed to be made during wet weather playtimes, as long as they weren't thrown – deliberately – at the teacher on classroom duty.

Fortune Teller

However, without a doubt, the most popular paper toy, and one which is still made by many schoolgirls today, was the 'Fortune Teller'. A square of paper was folded diagonally into a triangle, opened up and folded the other way, then opened up again. The resulting square had four creases, and the corners were then folded to the centre. The square was turned over and the process repeated. When the folding was complete, you ended up with an intriguing toy which moved when you inserted your fingers into the base, opening and closing them in a scissor movement. The fun bit was filling in the Fortune Teller with numbers, coloured dots, and best of all, the fortunes, which could be basic or extremely involved.

When I was at school during the early-1960s, some of us spent hours making these toys, going into incredible detail by decorating them with beautiful patterns and neat lettering. Sometimes they became mini works of art, covered in coloured swirls, flowers, spirals and stars. We would spend ages dreaming up the predictions but most of us were insistent that the fortunes were good or, at least, would give us hope. We never included anything about dying, tragedy, accidents or poverty. Fortune Tellers were often made in the playground, as well. A group of girls armed with paper and a pack of coloured pencils could while away many a playtime folding the paper, then working out the fortunes, adding the colours and numbers. Finally, we would play with them, getting each other to choose their colour, number and, eventually, to read their fortune.

Occasionally, we made such spectacular versions that we couldn't bear the thought of playing with them. We called these 'salt cellars' and proudly took them home where they were placed on the dining room table, either to contain loose salt (we were less enlightened about the causes of high blood-pressure in those days), or used as a holder for a cruet set. On the whole, though, it was the creating that was fun; once they were finished and we had tried them out on our friends a few times, the Fortune Tellers were discarded until the next wet playtime.

Future fortune

I've remembered the 'Fortune Teller'. It was a sort of Origami exercise as you had to take a sheet of paper (a square) and firstly write numbers – one to four in a clockwise direction along the edge and draw a picture or put a different coloured dot in each corner. Then, fold two opposite diagonal corners together, open it back up and then repeat this with the other two opposite diagonal corners. Open it back up again and then turn the paper over and fold all four corners to the centre of the paper. Turn the paper back over so that the pictures/numbers are face down. Then fold all four corners into the centre of the paper. Fold any two sides together and this should move the numbers to the inside with just the pictures on the outside. You could always write the numbers now rather than at the beginning if it's easier. Then you can slide your thumbs and fingers under the four flaps and you should be able to expand the Fortune Teller. Make sure you've written a message under each flap though to give different answers which could say things like 'You're lovely' or 'You'll marry a Prince' – or anything really!

The way to play it was to choose a colour, for instance blue, and then spell out the word opening the Fortune Teller one way on 'b', another on 'l' etc and then choose a number keeping the Fortune Teller open. Do the same thing but this time with the numbers and when finished counting open the flap under the number chosen and see what it says!

We spent ages doing this in the playground and I'd forgotten all about it! Some of the Fortune Tellers were really decorative too!

Sharon White, teaching assistant and involved with musical theatre

Still telling fortunes

We were still making fortune telling toys at school in the 1990s.

Jenna Brewer, born 1980, ballet and bunny enthusiast

A fortune teller and a paper boat – simple to make when you know how.

Hats and boats

Paper hats or boats were simple and quick to make. All you needed was a rectangular piece of paper (for a hat, a sheet of newspaper was ideal), and you folded the two short edges so they met. Then the left and right corners from the central creases were folded until their edges met. Next, the leftover lower edges on each side were folded up to make the brim (or the hull of the boat). Colouring and decorating them was a good way of passing the time, and was encouraged by teachers at our primary school because it was peaceful and allowed them to drink their tea and read their book without being pestered!

Paper water bombs

Water bombs were also great fun, but were not, of course, officially allowed, although a few of the more daring boys would fold these 'water-tight' boxes from paper and then fill them from the drinking water fountain in the cloakroom. The bombs could then be thrown across the playground or the Quad when no teachers were watching.

Nowadays, children don't carry hankies – once, they were a necessity.

Knickers to that

Vera would always bring me something back [from an outing]. I would try to stay awake till she came. If I was asleep, she would wake me and produce an apple or pear from her knicker leg and I would sit up in the darkness enjoying this special treat.

Joan Warne,
talking about her elder sister, Vera

HANDKERCHIEF GAMES

Before tissues caught on, everyone carried a handkerchief. Right up to the 1970s, they were an essential item. Children's hankies tended to be smaller than the adult ones, and were often prettily and colourfully decorated with nursery characters. Sometimes, a child had the hanky safety-pinned to their jumper, but normally they were stuffed into pockets or, in the case of girls, in the traditional hiding place of up a knicker leg.

Knicker legs, incidentally, were amazingly useful. They could store all kinds of treasures. I heard of one child, many years ago, who detested rice pudding, and managed to hide it up her knicker leg, while girls regularly used a knicker leg as a useful bag, with small toys, food, sweets and hankies all stuffed up there.

In the 1950s, some of the grey school knickers we had to wear had useful little pockets sewn onto them. They were just about big enough to take a hanky.

As they were always accessible, hankies were a useful adjunct to play, whether transformed into a 'pirates flag', waved as a signal of surrender, or used to shield a child from the hot sun. They were also wonderful for folding, with girls, especially, gathering in small groups to make things from their hankies.

Lady in an Accident

Lady in an Accident was an easy make. The hanky was folded diagonally into a triangle. Keeping the point at the top, the two corners were folded onto the top point, then the whole thing (now a diamond shape) was flipped over. Then the child said, 'A lady has had an accident. She's lying down. This is the lady's dress', (pointing to the top layer of the diamond). The 'dress' was lifted to reveal the next layer. 'This is the lady's petticoat.' Then the 'petticoat' was raised, to reveal the lower parts of two triangles. A triumphant cry of, 'And here are the lady's knickers!' finished the game. (Cheeky, a few decades ago!).

Considered really daring was making a bra from a hanky or a brassiere as we then called it. Actually, we referred to our intricate creation as 'a bow' and made a show of putting it on our heads, pretending to look shocked when friends giggled and whispered it was a brassiere. Children were so much more naïve in the 1950s!

Creatures could be fashioned from hankies if you were skilful enough, such as a rabbit, a baby, a ghost or a mouse. Some of the results were quite impressive, and once the basic folds and necessary steps were mastered, we could produce cute toys quickly, and our small, nimble fingers helped us to make the intricate creases much more easily than an adult could manage. We never were bored – we'd whip out our hankies which doubled up as a portable toy. Today's tissue-wielding children don't know what they are missing!

Twins in a Cradle
Twins in a Cradle was a particularly popular make and was quick and easy to do. Basically, the hanky was folded diagonally and then both corners were rolled into babies. One of the points was pulled upwards, the other downwards to form the cradle, with the babies tucked inside.

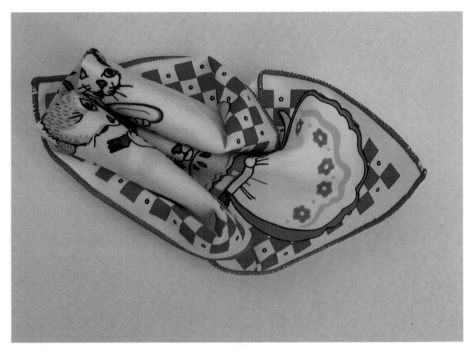

Twins in a cradle – with a bit of imagination!

OTHER RAINY DAY GAMES

Comics

Comics were always kept in our school satchels, so could be passed around on a rainy day. Beano and Dandy were favourites, while Schoolfriend, Bunty and Judy were popular too. Some 'upper class' children had Girl, a glossy, top of the market paper, and the boy's equivalent was The Eagle. They were all only too willing to swap them for a forbidden Beano! Later, we discovered Boyfriend comic, with its centrefold picture of up-to-the-minute pop stars such as Cliff Richard, The Beatles or Bobby Vee. This was a glossy, so fairly acceptable – Cherie, Roxy and similar 'poppy' girls' comics were not really approved of!

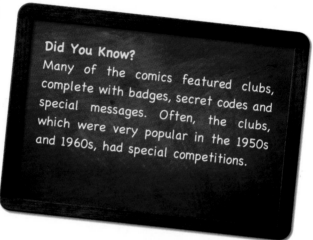

Did You Know?
Many of the comics featured clubs, complete with badges, secret codes and special messages. Often, the clubs, which were very popular in the 1950s and 1960s, had special competitions.

A pair of dice could be used for dozens of different games.

Dominoes

This family favourite is very old and is similar to a game played by the Chinese in the Twelfth Century. The first recorded European reference is in Italy, and it arrived in Britain, from France, in the late 1700s. Originally, the playing dominoes were made of thin bone and ebony, and there are 28 pieces in a standard set. Perfect for indoor play at school, the idea was to line up each domino so the same numbers touched e.g. four on one piece next to the four on another. However, children quickly learnt that a little patience was rewarded when they set the dominoes on their sides to form patterns which could be knocked over to create a falling display.

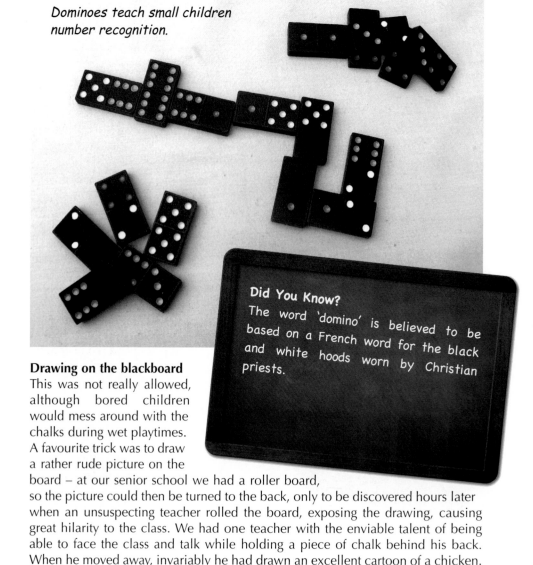

Dominoes teach small children number recognition.

Did You Know?
The word 'domino' is believed to be based on a French word for the black and white hoods worn by Christian priests.

Drawing on the blackboard
This was not really allowed, although bored children would mess around with the chalks during wet playtimes. A favourite trick was to draw a rather rude picture on the board – at our senior school we had a roller board, so the picture could then be turned to the back, only to be discovered hours later when an unsuspecting teacher rolled the board, exposing the drawing, causing great hilarity to the class. We had one teacher with the enviable talent of being able to face the class and talk while holding a piece of chalk behind his back. When he moved away, invariably he had drawn an excellent cartoon of a chicken. I always wished I had the skill to draw without looking.

French knitting

This became quite a craze at one time, and, in the days of wooden cotton reels, was cheap and cheerful. All you needed were four nails hammered into the top of the reel, and then you used lengths of wool to loop round the nails, forming stitches. Eventually, a knitted 'snake' would emerge through the hole in the bottom of the reel, and grow, and grow and grow.... and we never knew what to do with it after that. With hindsight, we should have coiled it and sewn it into hats and mats. Nowadays, as most cotton reels are plastic it is difficult to knock nails in, so would-be French knitters have to purchase a ready-made knitter from a toy or craft shop. It's still a good way of passing the time during a rainy day lunch hour, though.

Jigsaw puzzles

The very first jigsaw puzzles weren't intricately interlocking, as we know them today – they were cut into basic shapes. Today, these are known as dissected puzzles. They were made by pasting a picture onto a thin sheet of wood before being cut, and the pieces were just pushed into place, though occasionally a few might actually interlock. It's believed that John Spilsbury, from London, was the first person to make a dissected puzzle as a child's toy in the 1760s. He was an engraver and made his dissections of maps in order to assist the teaching of geography. A century later, treadle saws were introduced which enabled intricate, irregular shapes to be cut, and meant that puzzles could be interlocking (lessening the risk of them being inadvertently broken up by a sneeze or a nudge).

By the late 1800s, cardboard puzzles were also known, though they were mainly intended for children. In the Twentieth Century, these puzzles were die cut, using sharpened thin strips of metal in intricate shapes to stamp out the pieces, rather like a pastry cutter.

Jigsaw puzzles have always had a place in the classroom; infants' schools begin with the tray types which consist of a colourful board with one or more lift off shaped pieces, often revealing a different picture beneath. Simple basic two-piece or three-piece interlocking puzzles soon give way to more complicated puzzles as a child's skill increases. Most 'rainy day' cupboards at school contain puzzles, usually fairly small ones which can be completed within the allocated break time, though invariably there are a few larger ones donated by some kind parent having a clearout.

1950s puzzle – the school ones invariably had one piece missing.

Knitting

Lots of us took knitting needles and wool into school to occupy ourselves during playtime. Often, we would knit blanket squares for charity, though there were a couple of girls who had a crush on the PE teacher and were knitting him a pullover!

Mazes and related puzzles

These often consist of a small box with a glass or perspex top. Inside is a maze, picture, pegs or catches, and, usually several small holes. The aim is either to get a small ball bearing through a maze, to complete a picture by trapping ball bearings as eyes, buttons etc, or to get shapes – such as discs – trapped on pegs or under catches. Some of the maze games are very attractive, and there must be thousands of different kinds and types.

Other variations include those where the ball is trapped inside an opaque box and manoeuvred by sound alone, or games with larger wooden boards which the player rocks from side to side as they move the ball along intricate channels, avoiding the holes. The pocket-size mazes, in particular, are perfect for school play, as they are quite addictive and so will entertain a child all playtime. They also teach hand-eye co-ordination and thinking ahead to the next move.

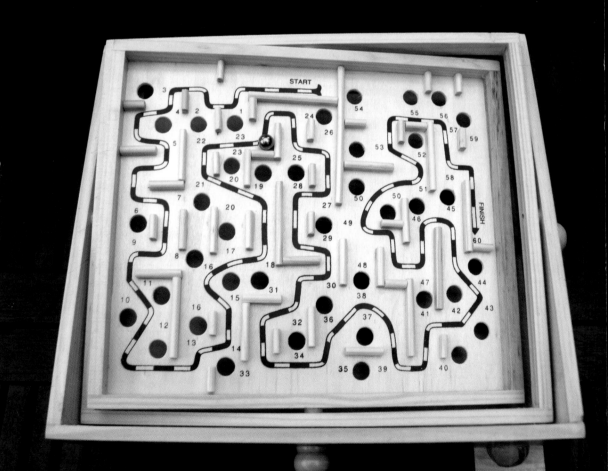

Portable pocket games – useful for instant play.

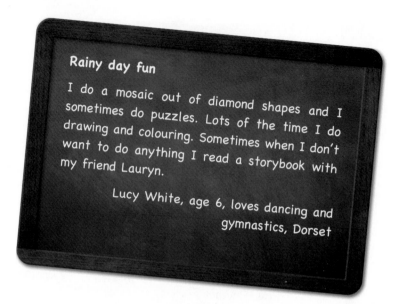

Plasticine

A school staple, Plasticine was created in 1897 by an art teacher, William Harbutt, who taught in a school near Bath and wanted a non-drying clay which his sculpture students could use. The resulting mixture of chalk, petroleum jelly and stearic acid has stood the test of time, being a non-toxic malleable product which won't dry on exposure to air, although it does harden somewhat. In 1900, commercial production started at a factory at Bathampton, and the original grey Plasticine was dyed and sold in four colours, though many other colours were soon available. In 1963, the factory was destroyed by fire, but was rebuilt and the Harbutt company continued to make the product in the same location till 1983. It is still marketed today, and has gained an army of followers inspired by Nick Park who used Plasticine in his Wallace and Gromit animated series, and, before him, by Tony Hart who modelled the TV character, Morph with it.

Tubs of Plasticine were always available for wet weather play when I was at school, and we would mould animals, fruit and people – the time really raced by. There was a ritual with Plasticine – when it came from the tub, it needed to be softened, and so we would warm it in our hot little hands, trying to squash and squish it till it became malleable. Strangely, although to start with it was in pretty shades of blue, red, orange, yellow and green, the colours soon merged together to become a uniform muddy brown. Plasticine had a distinctive smell, too, quite pleasant and instantly nostalgic.

Wool gathering

This pastime, a favourite amongst the girls in the late-1950s, was eventually clamped down on by mothers. It involved exactly what it says – gathering or plucking fluffy wool from each other's jumpers. Who started the craze, or why, I have no idea, but I do know that, at one point, we all carried around huge balls of fluff which we would pluck from each other's clothing. Girls who wore brightly coloured cardigans and sweaters were particularly vulnerable and, in the end, some girls had enormous fluffy multicolour balls. Then our mums realised that our knitwear was wearing thin, and the game was outlawed.

Raining in my heart

So many memories have been stirred up during the writing of this book and, strangely, one of the most recurring themes has been rainy days. Evocative memories of the smell of wet hair, soggy shoes, damp clothing, and the children being confined to the classrooms while longing to be outside in the playground splashing through the puddles – we can all remember the feeling.

Some schools run various clubs during the lunch breaks, which solves the rainy day problem, at least for members. I recall a wet week at school in the 1950s, when the enterprising music teacher announced a series of 'concerts' during the lunch hour. One day, she put a recording of Handel's *Messiah* on the record player, and dozens of us just sat on the hall floor to listen. Before she began, she simply announced, 'I intend to listen and enjoy. If you want to listen, you are welcome here. Anyone who dislikes the music can walk out – but I will have no talking or giggling.' Not one child walked out – Handel kept us enthralled, especially when the teacher allowed us all to join in the *Hallelujah Chorus*. I can't see that happening today with the *X-Factor* generation.

However, it was only pouring rain which kept us in; drizzle or the odd shower was nothing. We were sent out to play, while the teachers watched us, coffee cups in hand, through the windows of their snug staff room. If we really didn't like it, we were allowed to shelter in the 'lobbies' – the places outside each classroom where we hung our coats and left our outdoor shoes, which were equipped with plenty of wooden benches. It often built up a bit of a fug, and there was the smell of sweaty shoes from the racks, but there were coats to hide behind and benches to climb on. The hard floor was perfect for jacks. Let it rain!

We didn't mind. Children can find fun at playtime whatever the weather, wherever they are and whatever props are at hand. All they need is imagination – and, luckily, that's something every child is blessed with.

"School is over, O! what fun! Lessons finished, play begun;
Who'll run fastest you or I? Who'll laugh loudest? Let us try."

HOME FROM SCHOOL.

Acknowledgements

So many people have helped with this book that it would be impossible to mention them all. However, I'd like to say grateful thanks – in no particular order – to Sharon White, Holly White, Lucy White, Janet High, Kathy Martin, Amy Martin, the staff and pupils of White House School in Wokingham, the staff and pupils of Rushcombe First School in Corfe Mullen, Shelley Cuff, Eileen Lambert, Barry Carter, Local History Officer David Devine of Harlow Museum, Museum Education Officer Claire Hooper of Harlow Museum, Karen Conn, Mark Wynter, Lesley Glover, Mary Rippon, Brenda Newman of the Fernhurst Archives, Doris Howe, Edna Higgins, Tracy Martin, Trish Maunder, Keith and Margaret White of Mill Grove, Peter Andrews, Joan Kinnock, Michaela Clark, Margaret Follwell, Vicky Hooper, Jo Birch, Jill Jackson, Alison Sibley, Jayne Soule, Vivien Shortland, Kirsteen Macfarlane, Catriona Macleay, Gail Caberlon, Jean Needle, Lee Beaumont, Jeanette Nott, Marlene Hardesty, Marjorie Last, Chris Wimsey, Graham Warne, Michael Warne, Ben Wilkinson of Herts and Essex Newpapers and staff at the Welwyn Times. Also to Virtual Valley for permission to use quotes from *My Other Family* written by my late Mother, Joan Warne.

Finally, special thanks must go to my long-suffering family, especially to Malcolm, Simon and Jenna, who came under a constant barrage of questions regarding their school memories whenever they came into my line of vision!

PHOTO CREDITS

Brewer, Malcolm, *p98, 138, 144, 149, 150, 161, 162, 163, 164, 165, 166, 171, 172, 175, 176, 177, 178, 179, 182, 183.*

Fernhurst Archives, *p13.*

Harlow Museum, *p112 (upper).*

Jerles, Brenda, *p156.*

Martin, Kathy, *p10, 15, 22, 30, 51, 6, 70 (lower), 77, 81, 83, 92, 96, 101, 104,113, 114, 116, 119, 120, 128.*

Martin, Tracy, *p76.*

Mill Grove, *p2, 8, 18.*

Photograph on p11 taken from George R. Sims *Living London*, 1902.

Shoop, Fiona, *p21, 32, 45, 47, 50, 86, 160.*

Stacey's Auctioneers, *p141 (lower).*

White, Sharon, *p34, 57, 58, 102, 106, 108, 123, 125, 131, 133, 146, 147.*

Wicksteed Park, *p14.*

www.pachd.com, p58.

FURTHER READING

Davidson, Alexander, *Blaziers, Badges and Boaters* (Scope 1990)

Gross, Nigel and Pavely, Chris, *Hopscotch and Other Playground Games* (Parragon, 2002)

Kevill-Davies, Sally, *Yesterday's Children* (Antique Collector's Club Ltd. 1991)

May, Trevor, *The Victorian Schoolroom* (Shire Books, 1994)

Opie, Iona and Peter, *Children's Games in Street and Playground* (OUP 1969)

Opie, Iona and Peter, *The Lore and Language of Schoolchildren* (New York Review Books, April 2001)

Opie, Iona and Peter, *The Oxford Dictionary of Nursery Rhymes* (Oxford University Press 1997)

Roberts, Chris, *Heavy Words Lightly Thrown* (Gotham 2005)

Symonds, Jimmy, *Playground Games* (Henderson 1995)

Index

Accidents 13
Aeroplanes 172
All in Together Girls 115
Allee Allee in 69
Ally Ally-O 21
Alphabet Games 168
Ankle Skip Ball 151
Apple Pudding 52
Apples, Peaches 116
Appreciate 117
Arab Springs 68
Ask Me No Questions 89
Astragals 137

Baby Bumblebee 43
Bad Eggs 92
Baden-Powell 123
Ball 20, 91, 92, 95-100, 102, 149-151
Ball and cone 149
Ball Tag 95
Bats 20, 103, 150
Battleships 168
Beads 158
Beat Your Neighbour 165
Beggar My Neighbour 165
Biff bat 159
Bilbo Catch 148
Bilboquet 148
Blackboard 180
Blindman's Bluff 64
Blindman's Buff 64
Bluebell, Cockleshell 117
Boat race 151
British Bulldog 64
Bubble Car 117
Build a Bonfire 49

Bumps 131
Bye Baby Bunting 53

Call Ball 95
Can I Cross Your Shining River? 65
Cap rockets 151-152
Card games 165-166
Cartwheels 68
Catch a Falling Sputnik 48
Chain He 82
Charlie Chaplin 117
Charlie's Dead 86
Chess 160
Chewing gum 8
Chinese Whispers 65
Ching Chang Cholla 59
Cigarette cards 91, 147, 157
Circle Ball 95
Clapping 105
Coffee 118
Colour Touch 84
Colours 66, 120, 127
Comics 179
Conkers 12, 152
Consequences 169
Cowardy Cowardy Custard 87
Crab Game 66
Cry Baby Bunting 88
Cup and ball 148
Curiosity Killed the Cat 89
Cut His Hair 87

Daisy Chains 135
Dan Dan 87
Diabolo 145
Dibs 138

Dip a Penn'orth of Chips 56
Dip Dip Dip 53
Dipping 51-52
Do You Like Butter? 135
Dodge Ball 97
Dolls 8, 137, 151, 157
Dominoes 180
Don`t Care Was Made to Care 85
Donkey 97, 165
Dots and Boxes 171
Double Dutch 131
Double Skipping 131
Down by the Meadow 119
Down by the River 121
Down in the Valley 121
Draughts 161
Drill 18
Drop the Handkerchief 66
Duck, Duck, Goose 67
Dunce, Dunce, Double D 89
Dusty Bluebells 29
Dutch Girl 121

Each Peach Pear Plum 103
Eeenie Meenie Minie Moe 54
Eeeny, Meeny, Mackeracker 53
Egga 93
Elastics 132
England Was Hungary 85

Fairy 8, 123
Farmer's in the Dell 10, 22
Farmer's In The Den 23
Feignights 84
Feignlights 84
Film Stars 67
First the Worst 88
Fivestones 10, 20, 137
Flies in the Kitchen 123
Flu 123
Follow My Leader 67
Fortune Teller 60, 173
Free gifts 155
Freebies 155
French knitting 181
French skipping 131-132
Funny People 169

Giant Stride 13-14
Giddy Giddy Gout 88
Ginger You're Barmy 87
Girl Guide 123
Grandmother's Footsteps 68
Grottoes 135
Guess What 170

Ha Ha Ha 81, 89
Handel's Messiah 185
Handkerchief games 66, 177
Handstands 63, 68
Hangman 170
Happy Families 165
Have a Cigarette, Sir 54
Have You Ever, Ever, Ever 106
He 10, 12, 15, 81-82, 84, 95
He Loves Me 136
Here We Go Gathering Nuts in May 25
Here We Go Round the Mulberry Bush
25-28
Hickory Dickory Dock 53
Hide and Seek 16, 69
Hidey He 82
Higgedy, Piggedy 55
Higgeldy Piggeldy 55
Hoops 19, 145
Hopscotch 10, 12, 15-16, 69
Hula Hoop 145-146

I Beg Your Pardon 86
I Draw a Snake 72
I Gave Her Kisses One 31
I Had a Little Puppy 124
I Had a Sausage 124
I Know a Secret 89
I Saw Esau 122
I Sent a Letter 28
I Went to a Chinese Laundry 53
I Went to a Chinese Restaurant 107
Ibble Obble 57
Ice Slides 80
Ickle Ockle 56
Iggy Oggy 56
Iko, Iko 89
In and out the Window 30-31
Ink Pink Pen Ink 55

Inky Pinky Ponky 55
Ip Dip 56
Ippa Dippa Dation 56
Ippy Dippy 56
I-Spy 63, 72
It 81, 83, 93, 95, 97, 100

Jacks 20, 139-141, 185
Jane Austen 148
Jelly 124
Jigsaw puzzles 181, 160
Jimmy Jimmy Knacker 74
Jingle Bells, Batman Smells 49
Jump the Rope 133

Keeper of the Stones 74
Kings 84
Kingsys 84
Kingy 97
Kiss Chase 15, 74
Knicker Legs 176
Knife, Fork, Spoon, Spear 68
Knitting 182
Knucklebones 137

Lady in an Accident 177
Leapfrog 74
Letters 75
Liar, Liar 88
Lip-cutting grass 136
London Bridge is Falling Down 32
London's Burning 35
Looperoo 147
Lucy Locket 36
Ludo 162

Mabel, Mabel 124
Made You Look 87
Marbles 10-11, 15-16, 20, 91, 141
May We Cross Your Golden River? 65
Mazes 182
Melting Candles 82
Mickey Mouse 125
Milk time 8
Miss Polly 125
Moses 126
Mother, May I? 75

Mummy Thais I Listhp 87
Murder 75
My Bonnie Lies Over the Ocean 55
My Bunny Lies Over the Ocean 56
My Grandpa and Your Grandpa 89
My Mother Said 108
My Teacher's a Funny'un 48

Napoleon 144
Nebuchadnezzar 98
Nine Men's Morris 162
Noughts and Crosses 171

Old Maid 167
Old Roger is Dead 36-37
Oliver Cromwell Lay Buried and Dead 38
On the Mountain 38
One Little, Two Little, Three Little Indians 97
One Man Went to Mow 44
One Potato, Two Potato 57
One Two 59
One Two Three 57, 59
One Two Three and Plainsie 97
One, Two, Three O'Lary 97
Oom Pah Vee 108
Oranges and Lemons 10, 39
Origami 171

Paper aeroplanes 172-173
Paper boats 175
Paper darts 172-173
Paper folding 171-173
Paper games 167
Pat-a-Cake 108
Pease Pudding Hot 109
Peter, Peter Pumpkin Eater 127
Petticoat 86
Piggy in the Middle 99
Piggy on the Railway 62
Pincha, Puncha 62
Plantain guns 136
Plasticine 154, 189
Playground lady 9
Please, I've Come to Learn a Trade 75
Pogs 155

Pokemon 156
Poor Jenny is A-weeping 41
Poor Mary Sat A-weeping 41
Prams 8, 137
Puzzles 181

Queenie, Queenie 99

Rainbow Traffic Lights 79
Rainbows 78, 79
Rainy days 159, 185
Rat-a-Tat-Tat 61
Red Light, Green Light 78-79
Ring-a-Ring-o'-Roses 41
Rocket 151-152
Rubber dolly 127
Rubik's Cube 154

Salt, Mustard, Vinegar, Pepper 124, 131
Sausages 128
Scarlet, Scarlet 68
Scoubidou 147
See See My Playmate 109
Shipwreck 76
Simon Says 76
Skipping 10, 12, 15, 16, 111-135
Slammers 155
Snakes and Ladders 163
Snap 167
Snow 80
Solitaire 164
Spinning tops 20, 150
Spuddy 100
Squares 171
Stare Cat, Stare Cat 87
Statues 77
Sticky Toffee 82-84
Stone He 84
Stuck in the Mud 84

Tag 16, 81, 95
Teddy Bear 128
Television games 77
Tell Tale Tit 87
Ten Green Bottles 44
Tenses 100

Thatcher 8
The Yellow Rose of Texas 48
There Was an Old Man 62
There's Somebody Under the Bed 129
This Old Man 45
Three-legged Race 79
Tic-Tac-Toe 171
Tig 81
Tinker, Tailor 60
Tops 19-20, 50, 150
Toucher 84
Trading Cards 155
Traffic Lights 78-79
Trampoline 156
Twins in a Cradle 178
Two Ball 100
Two Little Dickie Birds 126, 169
Two, Four, Six, Eight 117

Under the Palm Bush 110

Veinlights 84
Vote Vote Vote 130

Water bombs 175
Waves 126
We Three Kings of Orient Are 49
Westerns 77
What's My Line? 77
What's the Time, Mr Wolf 79
What's the Time? 62
What's Your Name? 85
Wheelbarrows 80
When Susie Was a Baby 110
While Shepherds Washed 50
Whip and top 150-151
Whistle While You Work 49
Whizzers 151
Wild Horses 80
With My Hand 46
Wool gathering 184
Wounded Soldier 101

Yan, Tan, Tethera, Methera 53
Yo-Yo 143

Tower of Boys